F-4 PHANTOM

F-4 PHANTOM

Bill Gunston

CHARLES SCRIBNER'S SONS
NEW YORK

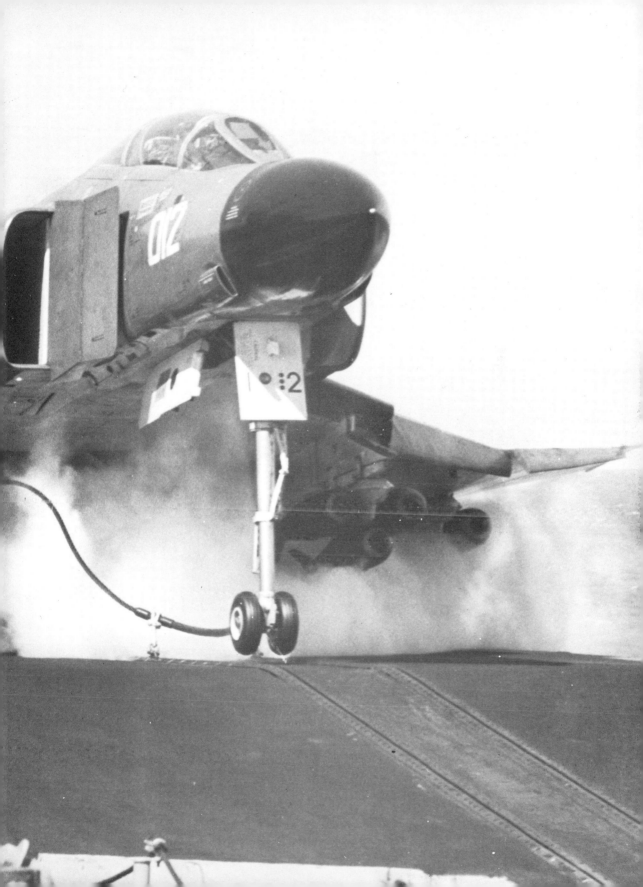

Printed in Great Britain
Library of Congress Catalog Card Number 77-77550
ISBN 0 684 15298 3

Contents

Left: A bomb laden US Air Force F-4C Phantom is shown here preparing to refuel from a US Air Force KC-135 tanker.

Introduction

When you have been a professional writer for 25 years you become very wary of describing anything as the first, or the biggest or the mostest. Even more dangerous is it to call something the best. But just now and again you get a feeling deep in your belly that overrides all the professional caution. One is human, after all. How could anyone possibly be clinically objective about the Phantom?

If there are such people, they may care to point out that, in the history of aviation, there have been fighters that are longer than the Phantom, or that have bigger wing-spans, or more engine thrust, or a higher top speed, or a greater gross weight, or perhaps even more ordnance (though I doubt the last item). I really do not wish to be reminded. As far as I am concerned, Mr Mac's Phantom is the mostest and the greatest and the best of its generation. To claim it was for more than ten years the standard against which other fighters were judged is no more than a plain statement of fact. To claim it has sustained the most successful programme of continued development and production of any aircraft in history is a very bold claim indeed, but I am prepared to put that too. A production run for 20 consecutive years (1958-78) costing, with spares, around twenty billion dollars is hard to equal.

Yet I can remember the day in May 1958 when I first clapped eyes on that rather grotesque shape. My colleagues and I on *Flight International* gathered round the fuzzy radioed news photo and started a highly critical running commentary: "Look at the size of the thing ... they must have got everything terribly wrong, and then tried to put it right; look at the way the outer wings are cocked up and the tailplanes cocked down, I've never seen anything like it. . .sheer brute force and ignorance, they'll do a four-engined fighter next . . ." — and so on. Though we had long since come to expect bold design from the St Louis company, this one really did seem to be a brutish monster. But some time later, after the Phantom had collected a shoal of remarkable world records, the

Editor of the journal dictated a leader devoted to the Phantom. In its previous 50 years the journal had never before published a leader about one type of aircraft. This one bore the title "McDonnell's Mostest".

It was at about this time that the US Air Force began to look very hard at the Navy's Phantom, because the fact that it was The Mostest was becoming inescapable. Already Douglas's Skyray and Chance Vought's Crusader had hiked the rival men in dark blue out of the back row and put them up at the front, right alongside the supersonic Air Force, and the traditional feeling of the Air Force that they ought to pity the Navy its compromised fighters with their inferior performance was fast being forgotten. But the Phantom was a real shaker. Could it possibly be that with this remarkable aircraft it was the men in light blue that were being pushed into the back row?

The very idea seemed ridiculous. How could a carrier-based aircraft, with all its problems of catapulting, folding, arresting, compatibility with the harsh marine environment, and a dozen other severe compromises, possibly surpass the best fighter designed to fly from a big Air Force base? Yet it began to look as if the Phantom was not just a bit better in one or two areas but much better all round. It had radar that outperformed the radar in the best Air Force interceptor. It had heavier missile armament, and greater versatility. It carried more bombs further than the best Air Force fighter/bomber or attack aircraft, and delivered them more accurately in all weathers. It flew further than any other fighter. It flew faster than any. It flew higher than any, and got up there quicker. It could also fly amazingly slowly, and was a pleasure to fly (if you kept to the book). It had two of everything, including two men in the crew, and seemed to have a better chance of coming home than the rival aircraft that had only one. Its safety record was unrivalled. Though one might draw superior things on paper, the Phantom was so good that, for the first time ever, a Navy fighter was bought by the Air Force.

It was also at this time that the then Secretary of Defense hit on the idea of "commonality" in aircraft designed for what appeared to be similar tasks, to save a sum which his staff in the Pentagon estimated at one billion dollars. The Navy wanted a Fleet Air Defense Fighter to replace the Demon and Crusader. The Air Force wanted a new advanced 'fighter' to replace all the Century-series fighter/bombers, interceptors and tactical reconnaissance aircraft. The resulting TFX programme gave rise to the F-111A for the Air Force and F-111B for the Navy. It was meant to sustain a huge multi-service, multi-nation programme that would make these the primary tactical aircraft of The Free World. But it did not work out that way. While the F-111 faltered, the Phantom went from strength to strength. Instead of being swiftly phased out of production, as was planned, this older aircraft was bought in bigger and bigger quantities, and by more and more customers.

It was fortunate for the United States that the Phantom happened when it did. Admittedly it was not the only plane in the sky. There were many naval aviators who claimed "When you are out of F-8s you are out of fighters". Others who flew from carriers and land bases said there was no attack bomber half so good as 'The Scooter' — Ed Heinemann's baby A-4 Skyhawk. In the Air Force many hundreds of men came to love the mighty iron hardware from Republic: the F-105 Thunderchief, affectionately known as The Thud. Even the fine old F-100 Super Sabre — The Hun — stayed valiantly in the front line doing every kind of job, and doing it very well. But the F-4 Phantom outperformed them all. It was in a class by itself — unfair competition that could take on every specialised aircraft and fly its missions even better. Before long its rivals, both older and newer, were falling by the wayside, while Phantoms poured out of the St Louis factory to take their place.

It was a matter of some importance, far transcending the rewards to Mr Mac's stockholders. In the 1960s, the Viet Cong — though never a direct menace to the United States — was trying every way it knew to take over the unfortunate land of South Vietnam. Terror and intimidation failed, and the only answer was frontal attack by military forces. For better or worse, the United States answered the call of the Saigon government for help, and thus became embroiled in a war of enormous magnitude and duration. When I was asked to write this book, in 1974, the Viet Cong had been held at bay, and no single weapon had done more to accomplish this than the Phantom. Today that seems a long time ago, and the former Phantom jocks are sad and disillusioned. Perhaps the outcome was inevitable, though one can argue endlessly about the rights and wrongs of this tragic and destructive war. In another theatre there is also room for argument, for in the beleaguered state of Israel the Phantom plays a front-line role in what is still a matter of life and death. Hopefully in this area the outcome will be happier, showing that the inhabitants of our planet do not have to try to kill each other. Perhaps the saddest of all man's many exhibitions of self-destruction was the 'war' between Greece and Turkey in Cyprus in the hot summer of 1974. Here two proud and intelligent people resorted to blows, despite the fact they have lived alongside each other from prehistoric times. Both belong to NATO, and both have squadrons of Phantoms.

When friend clobbers friend, the senselessness of coming to blows is especially obvious. I am not one to glorify war or laud man's achievements in armaments. Yet this book has a perfectly valid place on anyone's shelf. It is a pictorial record of the pre-eminent combat aircraft of modern times. The men who have gone to war in it have been defending something: territory, a way of life, their homeland. In every case they have been glad of the Phantom as a powerful weapon to resist aggression. It has hit targets on the ground. It has hit enemy aircraft in the air. It has flown through intense fire to bring back pictures with cameras, infrared linescan and side-looking radar. It has remained a front-line weapon for nearly twenty years, and is likely to go on for another twenty. If in its second twenty years it has no fighting to do, that will be the best possible reason for having it.

Haslemere, England, 1976   Bill Gunston

Acknowledgements
Many people contributed to this book, but I would like especially to thank Norm Malayney of Winnipeg, Maj Shelton A. Goldberg USAF, Lt-Col Mark E. Berent USAF Rtd., Lt Timothy E. Prendergast USN, Herman Barkey, N. Gordon Le Bert and Geoffrey Norris of McDonnell Douglas and Henning Marks of Washington DC.

7

Background to the Design

In the United States, most combat aircraft have their origin in a requirement stated by one or more of the user services. If they go into production it is usually because they have not only met the requirement but also beaten the opposition either in a design competition or in an aerial 'fly-off'. But the Phantom's birth was quite different. McDonnell began the design of the Phantom because it lost out to the opposition; and there was no requirement for the Phantom by any of the US armed forces!

This doggedness was typical of the company which was founded by James S. McDonnell on July 6, 1939 on the second floor of a small building adjacent to St Louis Municipal Airport (Lambert Field). McDonnell Aircraft Company — called Mac from its initials, though its official abbreviation is MCAIR — had scanty resources, but brains and guts. At the start, Scots-descended McDonnell had to struggle to find the $100 a month rental for the office, and pay his staff (his secretary). His company was just beginning to get into its stride when World War 2 began. Its one important asset was that, having no traditions, it could tackle the new problem of jet propulsion as easily as those of propeller aircraft. In January 1943 the growing team received an order for a jet fighter to operate from the US Navy's aircraft carriers. This aircraft, the XFD-1, flew on January 25, 1945, and was the first naval jet aircraft to fly. The production article — Mac's first successful homegrown product — was the FH-1 Phantom. From it was developed the much more powerful F2H Banshee. First flown in 1947, the Banshee was a major success and 895 were built.

By this time the company's design team was busy with aircraft that were alike only in being bold and unlike anything done before. There was the XF-85 Goblin, a tiny jet fighter that was designed to drop out

Right: The original McDonnell FH-1 Phantom, the world's first carrier jet fighter./*USN*

8

9

Above: The futuristic but underpowered XF-88 of October 1948./*MCAIR*

Centre left: The F3H (later F-3) Demon of August 1951./*MCAIR*

Below left: First of the many: the prototype McDonnell F4H-1 on the runway at Lambert-St Louis Airport. First flown on May 27, 1958, this historic aircraft carried four dummy Sparrow missiles./*MCAIR*

of a B-36 bomb bay and defend its parent! In contrast, the XF-88 Voodoo was the longest fighter ever built at that time, as well as potentially the fastest; it looked as if someone had built the sketch of a visionary who could see the future. The XHJD-1 Whirlaway was a twin-engined helicopter with side-by-side intermeshing rotors. The JD-1 Little Henry was a tiny helicopter with the rotor driven by tip ramjets. The XV-1 was the world's first true V/STOL convertiplane. The carrier-based F3H Demon, first flown in August 1951, survived the total technical failure of its engine and, redesigned with a new engine, became a great success as the first fighter armed with guided missiles. In October 1954 the name Voodoo was resurrected for the F-101, which carried on the tradition of the original Voodoo of being the longest and fastest fighter flying. Unlike the underpowered earlier Voodoo it had the most powerful engine available — not just one, like the F-100 and Crusader, but two! An early F-101 set a world speed record at 1 207mph, and 807 were built for the US Air Force, some being passed on in 1961 to the Canadian Armed Forces.

With the Demon and Voodoo McDonnell establish-ed a reputation second to none in the field of advanced all-weather fighters — possibly the most difficult category in aircraft design, which some would say is in any case the most difficult human occupation. The company's aerodynamics, structures and systems capabilities were quite outstanding, and enabled success to be achieved in a most convincing and com-petent way with projects that outwardly looked daun-ting if not even frightening. But the rivals offered tough competition. In May 1953 the apparently vital award of the contract for the US Navy's first supersonic fighter went to Chance Vought in Texas. Mac's team were temporarily dejected, but they remained keenly aware of the fact that they too were good. They knew a lot about Navy fighters, and they boldly decided not to give up. What could they do in such circumstances? The St Louis management and engineers coolly decid-ed to go ahead in the absence of a customer and design a fighter that was later and better.

As Vought had won the supersonic day fighter Mac had to do something different. They talked to everyone in the Navy prepared to listen, in the hope of gathering together enough scraps of ideas to guess the kind of fighter that might be wanted in the next generation. From the Chief of Naval Operations (CNO) down through the Head of the Fighter Branch (at the time, Cdr Ralph Weymouth) to the big teams in the Bureau of Aeronautics (BuAer) and the Overhaul and Repair facilities, the engineers from St Louis stuck their feet in doorways, left questionnaires on desks, and invited anybody who would come to visit the company plant. Gradually the Navy's thinking was translated into the F3H-G project study, which in turn was the basis of a full-scale mock-up constructed in early 1954. It could not be a detailed engineering mock-up, because there was no engineering design in existence. But it was im-pressive, nonetheless.

Named Phantom II, it was an all-can-do proposal. It was outwardly rather like a cross between the Demon and the Voodoo, having the broad high-lift wing and multiple stores pylons of the former and the twin engines and highly supersonic performance of the latter. In the nose was a single-seat cockpit and a powerful radar. Below were four 20mm guns. Spread under wings and fuselage were no fewer than eleven hard points and pylons for carrying every store but one in the carrier-based naval armoury. Power came from two Wright J65 (Sapphire) engines, with which in the clean condition a high-altitude Mach number of at least 1·5 was expected. A higher figure was thought possible, because the engine inlets were to have variable geometry, for peak engine performance at all speeds and heights. Much effort went into this new feature, and into attempts to avoid pitch-up by putting the horizontal tail low down. Rather to McDonnell's

surprise, in November 1954 the BuAer signed a letter of intent for two aircraft, to be designated AH-1, similar to the mock-up but powered by the new General Electric J79 engine when this became available. But it was not necessarily the start of a proper programme; the Navy had no requirement for any such aircraft, and the award was intended primari-ly to investigate possibilities and to keep the valued design team from breaking up. Work went ahead, and the first hardware was cut on system rigs and tunnel models, but the Navy was unable to write a definitive specification.

Work drifted on as best it could, though it was clearly imprudent to begin detailed engineering design. Then in April 1955 four officers, two from BuAer and two from CNO, came to St Louis and in sixty minutes flat had outlined what they wanted. They gave the programme purpose and direction, and it was not the direction expected. It was not to be an AH-1 (multi-role attack) at all, but a fighter. The Navy wanted a fleet defence fighter that could fly out 250 nautical miles, stay on CAP (combat air patrol) two hours, destroying any enemy aircraft that might come along, and return to the deck after a three hour mission. Within the following two weeks much happened. The AH-1 was torn apart, both on paper and in the mock-up. The J65 engines were pulled out and replaced by the more powerful J79. The guns were pulled out and replaced by guided missiles in the form of four big Sparrows carried in a novel semi-submerged way under the wide flat-bottomed fuselage. This was a good compromise solution, giving very little drag yet oc-cupying only a fraction of the volume of a missile bay inside the fuselage. Each missile was arranged to be ejected downwards by explosive charges, its motor ig-niting about a half-second later. Choice of the Sparrow automatically dictated the basic form of radar fire-control, which by this time was well "down the road" at the Westinghouse Air Arm Division at Baltimore, to illuminate the target for the missile to home on the reflected radiation. Ten of the eleven hard points were eliminated (later eight were put back), leaving only a centreline rack for a large drop tank. After 14 hectic days and nights a completely new detail specification was written and approved. It was no longer the AH-1; the Phantom II had become the F4H-1 fighter. This specification was refined in the F4H-1F document of July 1955 on which the prototypes were based.

As well as fundamental changes there were hun-dreds of secondary alterations. The switch to the more powerful J79 engines necessitated considerable enlargement of the air inlets and ducts, which now became narrow passageways filling almost the entire depth of the fuselage. Great care was taken to make the ducts to an exact profile, precisely repeatable on successive aircraft, and they were given a machined

11

inlet leading edge and heavy chem-milled skins supported by close-pitched ribs. To reap the fullest reward from the increased thrust the inlets were made variable, for the first time on any fighter. The inner face of the inlet is a sharp-edged fixed ramp, more than two inches out from the fuselage to allow the sluggish boundary-layer of air to escape. This huge flat wall has ever since been a characteristic feature of the Phantom. The sloping fixed ramp is followed by a more sharply inclined pivoted ramp, which at supersonic speeds compresses the airflow through an oblique shockwave and closes up the inlet as a function of total temperature of the airflow. Boundary layer on the ramps is sucked out through a vertical slit between them, and through 12 500 perforations in the movable ramp, to be discharged through louvres on top of the aircraft. Not all the remaining air goes through the engine: a by-pass flow, governed according to Mach number in the duct, discharges through bellmouth nozzles surrounding the engine jets. Large doors were added in the undersides of the ducts, opened by rams on take-off and at other times when full power is needed at low forward speed, and balanced against hydraulic springs so that they can blow open in the event of sudden throttle closure or compressor stall at high IAS (indicated air speed). This engine installation was outstandingly advanced for the mid-1950s, and was the main factor in allowing M max to be raised from 1·5 to over 2·5 — even today an exceptional speed.

The wing was substantially altered. The outer folding panels were extended in chord by ten per cent, giving a large "dog-tooth", and tilted up at a sharp 12° dihedral angle to increase stability. Boundary-layer control was greatly augmented by blowing hot compressor-bleed air along the leading-edge droop flaps as well as ahead of the short-span but very broad trailing-edge flaps. Lateral control is by inboard ailerons and spoilers immediately ahead of them; to roll, one spoiler goes up and the aileron on the opposite wing goes down. The vertical tail was extended in chord, making it the longest from front to rear on any fighter. The stabilator — the one-piece slab serving as the tailplane (stabiliser) and elevators — was tilted down on each side, first at 15° and then at a startling 23°, to get it out of turbulent wing wake at high angles of attack and counter the rolling effect of the outer wings in yawed flight. The main gears were stressed for carrier recovery at 33 000lb at a sink rate of 22ft per second. The nose gear was arranged to extend 20ins for catapult launch, and, for the first time on a fighter, provided with 360° power steering. The adoption of a new Westinghouse radar, the APQ-50 Mod derived from the Aero-13, dictated a longer and slightly fatter nose. Length at this time had to be held to less than 56ft to allow the aircraft to go down the centre deck lift (elevator) of *Midway*-class carriers. Though changes in carrier design soon eliminated this need, it resulted in the Phantom being extremely carefully packaged into a more compact airframe than might otherwise have been the case.

Extensive changes were also made to the 'black boxes' of the autopilot, fire-control system and other avionics, and nearly all were made more accessible. The complete radar was designed to be run out on rails for all-round access without removal from the airframe. The Navy kept its options firmly open as regards multi-role employment by standardising on a crew of two, in tandem cockpits, though it left dual controls as an unfitted option. The second seat displaced 125 gallons (150 US gal) of fuel, which accordingly caused the centreline tank to be enlarged from 375 to 500 (600 US gal). A folding flight refuelling probe, taking 1 700lb per minute, was added on the right side of the cockpits. Very important to the Phantom's future development, though the air-to-ground mission had become secondary, this was given most careful consideration by McDonnell engineers and eventually, without significant penalty to the clean aircraft, nine hardpoints were provided for a total external load of 16 000lb.

On May 26, 1955 McDonnell Aircraft was authorised to proceed with the newly defined XF4H-1 fighter, going ahead at full speed with detail design and manufacture of the two prototypes previously the subject of a letter of intent as AH-1s. But, partly owing to the rather large elements of risk and cost in the programme, the Navy decided also to buy a competing aircraft. Such a procedure provided a back-up insurance against technical failure of the first

programme, allowed the evaluation of contrasting solutions to the same requirement and, above all, kept the industry on its toes in a way that would be impossible without such competition. Competition within one nation's industry is not, as some British politicians seem to think, something merely wasteful. The rival award went to Chance Vought, whose submission was styled XF8U-3 Crusader III—suggesting a mere modification of the existing Crusader, then called XF8U-1, whereas in reality it was a totally new design. It was extremely fast, but had one seat, one engine, and carried less ordnance than the Phantom II. The first XF4H-1 flew at Edwards AFB on May 27, 1958. There it completed its contractor's flight trials, and then entered a hard-fought Navy Preliminary Evaluation against the first of five F8U-3s. The so-called 'Crusader III' was good, but ultimately the Navy preferred two seats and two engines. In December 1958 the BuAer awarded a limited contract for 23 development Phantom IIs (this total included the two already flown) plus 24 production aircraft.

In the course of development the engines were improved, probe/drogue flight refuelling incorporated, the full boundary-layer blowing installed, an infra-red scanner added in a fairing under the new bulged and pointed radome, and a rack added under each wing to carry two infra-red Sidewinder missiles or a single Sparrow. Thus equipped, the production machine was styled F4H-1F, but by the time the Phantom II entered service in quantity the new Department of Defense numbering system had been introduced. Instead of the Navy and Marine Corps aircraft being called F4H and the Air Force versions F-110, as was the case in 1961-63, it was decided to make the whole

family the F-4. Strictly, the Roman II should still be added after the name Phantom, but as there is no possibility of confusion I will from this point on omit it.

Thus the first production machine was called F-4A. From the very start it was a winner, and it entered service with very few engineering changes and an almost complete absence of controversy. New military aircraft have to meet certain standardised guarantees, such as M_{max}, ceiling, specific range (distance flown on a given mass of fuel), rate of climb, and empty weight. Most aircraft chalk up some minuses and some pluses, and with luck they come out just on the plus side. But the Phantom consistently exceeded its guarantees, and the sum of all the percentages was an unprecedented 75 per cent on the plus side. It was only natural that the excited customer's pilots should have a go at some world records.

Below left: Nice shot of one of the first F-4Bs about to be recovered on February 7, 1962. The aircraft belongs to VF-74 and the ship is probably *Saratoga./USN*

Below: Deck crew cluster round the exciting newcomer as F-4A No 6 thrusts gently forward on to No 2 catapult on USS *Independence* (CVA-62) during carrier suitability trials on February 17, 1960. This was the first time a Phantom was embarked. The small nose and flush canopy make the A model visually different from the Phantoms this deck crew were soon to know so well./*USN*

Every one a Record

cool the engines, modifications to improve performance or safety were trivial or non-existent.

The Navy chose to kick off by having a go at the world record for absolute altitude, then held by the Soviet Union at 94 658ft. It laid on Operation Top Flight in the course of the final phase of Phantom flight testing at Edwards in preparation for Fleet Trials in 1960. On December 6, 1959 Cdr Lawrence E. Flint Jr took off solo in a YF4H-1 prototype fitted with a barograph which had been inspected and sealed by the NAA representative. The aircraft was clean and did not have maximum internal fuel. Flint levelled off at a height just under 50 000ft which, according to computer calculations, offered the best level from which to trade speed for altitude. With the throttles wide open, the big fighter accelerated until it reached a level speed considerably in excess of Mach 2. At maximum speed, Flint sought and obtained ground clearance for a ballistic zoom. Pulling back on the stick with a nicely judged firmness he held just the right g until the Phantom was pointing almost straight up, with the engines still on full power. The sky at the zenith, in front of the windscreen, swiftly became deeper blue, dark violet blue and then almost violet-black. Flint felt like an astronaut; as he eased the stick forward he became weightless, and he saw that the horizon was noticeably curved. The haze layer he had passed through near the tropopause had dropped 12miles below. The willing J79s eventually flamed-out in the near-vacuum, and Flint closed the throttles. With supreme judgement he now kept pushing the stick further and further forward to maintain weightlessness, as the speed fell to below 45mph TAS — with literally 'nothing on the clock'. Still weightless he went over the top, the nose plunged down, and from then on it was mainly a rather tricky job of keeping the aircraft pointing the way it was going, as it re-entered the atmosphere and fell like a stone.

In denser air Flint relit the engines and made a normal recovery 40 minutes after take-off. His barograph recorded a peak altitude of 98 557ft. No 1 was in the bag.

The next record, set by the Marine Corps, was for speed round a 500 kilometre (about 310mile) closed circuit. The circuit can be flown at high altitude, the main stipulation laid down by the FAI being that competitors must exit from the course at an altitude at least as great as that at the entry. On the other hand, the departure does not have to be made in the same direction as the entry, so for the chosen triangular course over the Mojave desert it is possible to fly three straight sides whilst going round only two corners.

The Phantom started its life as the exclusive property of the US Navy and Marine Corps. Thanks to competition between the various branches of the US armed forces it is seldom long before test pilots, evaluation pilots, squadron commanders or even senior staff officers come round to considering what new equipment they have that might take a world record. The US Navy and Marine Corps have never been backward in this, and the Skyray and Crusader had given the process a tremendous fillip with some speed and climb records that gained international publicity. This was nice while it lasted, but logic suggested that the rival Air Force should soon win the records back again. So it proved, and the F-101, F-104 and F-106 took speed and climb records while, disturbingly, other world speed and climb records went to new supersonic aircraft of the Soviet Union. But the huge, jagged and brutish Phantom was turning in wholly exceptional performance figures in its test and evaluation flying at Edwards Air Force Base, California, and Patuxent River, near Washington DC. It did not look like a record breaker — not if one expected such aircraft to be small, slender and graceful. But piles of documents and computer tape attested to the fact that the Phantom was a truly phenomenal aircraft.

During 1959 discussions were held in Washington and at Edwards with a view to bringing this fact home to all concerned. The obvious answer was a series of world records, officially observed by the National Aeronautic Association (NAA) to meet the rigid rules of the international governing body, the Fédération Aéronautique Internationale (FAI). Thus began a succession of record flights which have no parallel in history. No other type of aircraft has ever gained so many diverse world records. What makes the achievement of the Phantom all the more remarkable is that each record was gained by an aircraft essentially unchanged from the combat-ready multi-role aircraft then in production. Except for the Operation Skyburner dash, which required water-injection to

Right: An F-4B echelon of VF-101, the second user of the Phantom which began with the original F-4A in 1961. The nearest machine (148369) is one of the original Block 1 production batch./*MCAIR*

Even for a Phantom, it takes planning to fly the best 500km record. One must begin with centreline and wing tanks, use their fuel first and drop them at the correct places and times. The start of the full-power run with afterburner must be judged exactly right, the altitudes and rates of change of altitude must be watched carefully, and the turn points and rates of turn must also be judged with precision. The course itself must be run flat-out, but no corner dare be cut and the finish height must be watched with particular care. Lt-Col Thomas H. Miller had plenty to occupy his mind as he took off, solo, in a Navy F4H-1 (F-4A) on September 5, 1960. Climbing out of Edwards at a gross weight of 49 500lb he held military (maximum dry) power to a height of 38 000ft. He reached this altitude over the desolate Salton Sea, dropped the wing tanks and turned left at Mach 0·8 to head for the start gate. At a distance of 150 miles he lit the 'burners and accelerated at full power. Ideally he would have liked to go straight ahead into the speed course, dropping the centreline tank early enough for the speed to build up to the maximum before the start gate, but not even the Mojave Desert course could offer sufficient territory for this to be possible. Instead, to avoid an inhabited area, Miller had to keep the big tank until he was a mere 30 miles from the gate, at 48 000ft at Mach 1·6, and then go into a tight right turn to the gate.

At the start, Mach number was 1·76 and the height 42 200ft. At full power, speed built up to 2·04 at 50 000ft at the first turn, and Miller had to pull gently round in a near-vertical bank to avoid cutting the corner yet avoid excessive drag due to g in the turn. He dropped 1 000ft on the shortish second leg, entering the second turn at Mach 2·05, and then went full bore for the finish, crossing the invisible exit gate at 46 000ft at 2·10. Miller deliberately gained 4 000ft; he

was taking no chances of being disqualified. Likewise he flew a total distance of 334 miles to make sure he did not cut the corners, and this is very close to the theoretical minimum distance allowing for the radius of turn at the two corners. The time from gate to gate was 15min 19·2sec, giving a speed for the record-book of 1 216·76mph. Actual speed, reckoned on the distance flown of 334miles, was over 1 305mph, and the total flight amounted to 776miles. Not least of the remarkable feats was an afterburner full-power run of 25½ mins, testifying to the Phantom's unprecedented long-range interception capability.

Three weeks later, on September 25, 1960, Cdr J. F. Davis USN made an attempt on the 100km (62mile) closed-circuit record. The old FAI rules merely stipulated that the course had to be entered after flying level, or climbing, for at least 1 000metres (3 280ft), and that no height should be lost between entry and exit gates. To fly the course in a Phantom it is necessary to use up at least 100 miles working up speed; then the aircraft must be rolled into a tight turn and held there, pulling a rather tiring 3g all the way round. It is impossible to fly a supersonic 100km circuit of any shape other than a circle, unless one is not trying to set a record. In fact the 100km circuit at Edwards is laid out around 12 points, but it is not really worth while to try to fly the course as truly 12-sided at Phantom speed.

Davis climbed to approximately 46 000ft for the best combination of speed and turning power, the Phantom being accurately plotted by radar and theodolites as in all modern world records under FAI observation. He set course accurately with wings level to intersect the circular course along a tangent, climbing gently with full afterburner to full speed at optimum height. On reaching the tangent point he rolled 70° to the left and entered his 3g turn. This had to be

maintained with great precision through 360°, leaving at an altitude greater than that at the entry. Davis completed the orbit in 2min 40·9sec, giving an official average speed of 1 390·24mph. In fact, of course, the speed was considerably higher. The 100km distance is calculated by adding together the 12 straight sides. The theoretical minimum distance the Phantom could fly was 102km, and the distance round the slightly larger circle actually flown was 104·9km, giving a true average speed of 1 459mph (equivalent to Mach 2·24). This was further proof of the Phantom's ability to manoeuvre accurately at extremely high speeds and to attack evasive targets.

The year 1961 was the 50th anniversary of US Navy aviation, and record-breaking figured prominently in the festivities — thanks to the Phantom. To start the ball rolling, on May 24, 1961 the Navy arranged a transcontinental dash from California to New York. Five F-4B Phantoms with combat crews were detached for the operation, two of them back-up spares. All five took off at timed intervals from Ontario Field, east of Los Angeles, and headed for New York, 2 446miles away. The technique was to climb in military power to 38 000ft, accelerate with afterburner to maximum speed at 50 000ft and, after a full-power dash at that level, let down to subsonic rendezvous with an AJ-1 Savage tanker at 35 000ft over New Mexico. With fuel replenished, the flight continued at over Mach 2 at 50 000ft before a second tanker rendezvous over Missouri. After a third afterburner dash a third inflight refuelling took place over Ohio. A fourth full-speed run at over 50 000ft then brought the aircraft overhead an observer with the necessary instrumentation at Floyd Dennett Field, NY.

The two back-up aircraft were not needed. The first of the three competing aircraft was flown by Cdr J. S.

Lake, with Lt (jg) E. A. Cowart as radar intercept officer (RIO) — which was then still quite a new flying trade in the Navy, replacing that of radar operator. They set a new record of 3hr 5min. But the second aircraft, flown by Cdr L. S. Lamoreaux with Lt T. J. Johnson as RIO, set a better record at 2hr 50min. This staggering figure seemed certain to be the final best, but the third aircraft, flown by Lt R. F. Gordon with Lt (jg) B. R. Young as RIO, set a time of 2hr 48min. This time, equivalent to a start-to-pass average of over 869mph, won the third crew the Bendix Trophy. The operational capability to which McDonnell pointed on this occasion was fast long-range deployment.

On August 28, 1961 came Operation Sageburner, which attempted to break the world record for absolute speed over a 3km course at low altitude. It had been set in an F-100 in 1953, and nobody had found the machinery — or guts — to do better than that subsonic mark. Flying a powerful jet fighter through the dense, turbulent air at low level is no joke. Even if the pilot avoids the infinitesimal error in stick position that would turn his mount into a ball of blazing fragments in a split second, the very roughness of the

Below left: Getting the feel of their new mount are a crew from VMF(AW)-314, the first Marine Corps squadron to receive the Phantom in early 1962./*USMC*

Below: In August 1962, when this photograph was taken, the US Navy had no heavy bomber that could rival the F-4B fighter's bomb load. In fact a 500lb low drag Mk 82 bomb actually weighs 580lb, so 24 total 13 920lb. Performing the feat are the first Phantoms to reach VF-41 (USS *Independence*)./*USN*

ride is a stern test of both man and machine. But in 1961 men and a machine were available that could set a new mark — not just marginally better but well up into the supersonic regime.

The Sageburner aircraft was an F-4A, flown by Lt Huntington Hardisty, with Lt Earl H. DeEsch as RIO. They had spent weeks studying the speed course, laid out at Stallion Sight, a valley on the vast White Sands Missile Range in New Mexico. Though the 3km (1·8mile) speed course itself was fairly flat, the surrounding terrain was hard and inhospitable. On the west side lay the Rio Grande river. To the south and east were 10 000ft mountain ranges. To the north was a mountain range rising to well over 10 000ft. Hardisty and De Esch had a real challenge in navigation, racing at fantastic speed right down 'on the deck' over the very solid terrain whilst complying with the FAI rules, which were written in the 'stick and string' era. One of these stipulated that at no time in the flight could a height of 500m (1 640ft) above the ground be exceeded. The height during the record runs must not exceed 100m (328ft). The course is only 1 000m (3 280ft) wide, and the aircraft must keep within it throughout each run. And a successful aircraft must make four runs through the traps, two in each direction. Attack pilots will agree this is close to the limit of what is possible even today; in 1961 it was even harder, for there were no autopilot-linked terrain-following radars, and the F-4A had no inertial system. Hardisty had to judge it all by eye, and fly manually.

He took off from Holloman Air Force Base and curved round to the left away from the speed course, 55miles distant, and headed for a point aligned with the course but about 60miles south of it. He and DeEsch shared the workload, but in many practice

flights they had become accustomed to supersonic navigation at terrain clearances varying between 1 000ft and about 100ft and they hit the turn entry on the nose. With full afterburner they pulled round to the left in a tight turn to come on to the speed course heading. They flew the course to the north, broke right and came back in a wide sweep, flew the course to the south and then repeated the whole exercise again. On the speed runs Hardisty held a height above ground of 125-175ft, the Phantom jarred by the sharp blows of thermals and turbulence, with the instruments little more than a blur. The mean of the four runs was 902·769mph, equivalent in the hot air to about Mach 1·25. Nobody has ever beaten this performance, which undoubtedly attests to a lot of guts and skill. It has less relevance to ground-level attack capability, which depends more on protective avionics at subsonic speeds with external ordnance.

On November 22 1961, two years after the Phantom might first have attempted the king of all records, Operation Skyburner was at last mounted. The chosen pilot was Marine Lt-Col Robert B. Robinson, flying solo. He was the lucky man selected to strap on the finest fighter in the world and write his name in the pages of fame in the one record that is instantly intelligible to all: the world record for absolute speed. In 1954 the FAI had at last agreed that the old rules specifying a 3km course flown at lower than 500m were archaic and dangerous. New rules were drafted allowing the record to be set by two passes in opposite directions over a 15/25km (9½/15½mile) course at high altitude, by far the most difficult requirement being the need to hold altitude within 100m (328ft) from the outer marker to the finish gate, a distance of 20 miles in one direction and 17 miles in the other. This

very severe test of pilot skill, likened to threading a small-eyed needle (and having to be right first time), had earlier negated numerous attempts by the US services to beat the 1956 record set by Peter Twiss of Britain, even though some of the American fighter aircraft were faster. Now Robinson had the fastest of all, and the task was primarily one of precision flying.

The Marine colonel took off from Edwards using afterburner, with a 500gal centreline tank and two 308gal wing tanks. He had to fly a perfect pattern, both in space and velocity, to try to accelerate straight ahead for the record course early enough to be at maximum speed before reaching the start gate, with full internal fuel. Unfortunately he had to compromise the mission to let go the tanks in safe unpopulated areas, and this gave insufficient distance for acceleration to be completed before reaching the course. A further problem was the stipulation that the acceleration must be done in level or climbing flight; and any vertical excursion greater than 500m (1 640ft) from the height at which the aircraft entered the range would result in disqualification. Robinson climbed to 33 000ft burning external fuel, using military thrust for the final part of the climb. He then dropped the centreline tank and lit the 'burners, accelerated to 1·3 and continued climbing. The wing tanks were dropped at Bristol Dry Lake range, 90miles east of the start gate, at entry altitude of 45 000ft and Mach 1·3. Holding full burner, Robinson saw the Mach needle creep round to 2·45 over the outer marker, and hit 2·57 in the few seconds it took to reach the finish gate. At once he came out of burner and let speed bleed off to make the turn back on course. He turned slightly left and kept that heading for over 100miles, before adding power abeam of Point Mugu — the Navy Pacific Missile

Above left: Operation Sageburner was flown by an F-4A with flush canopy and small nose but equipped with the infra-red seeker. It set a record of nearly 903mph at a height of about 150ft which has not been broken in the past 16 years./*USN*

Above: F-4A (F4H-1) No 142260 is hardly ever illustrated, yet it is probably the greatest Phantom of all. Piloted by Marine Col Bob Robinson, seen here just after the event, it gained the world record for absolute speed at over 1606mph in 1961./*MCAIR*

Range — and pulling round to the right. This time there was no problem about dropping tanks, and Robinson rolled out of the turn in full burner with 105 miles in which to accelerate. This time he hit the start gate at over Mach 2·5, and made the run at least 50mph faster, finishing at over 2·62.

Robinson's mean speed was 1 606·3mph, equivalent to almost Mach 2·6. He was using the second YF4H-1 prototype, fitted with a water/alcohol spray in the engine inlet ducts to cool the incoming air ahead of the compressors. Apart from this simple addition, the Phantom was not merely standard but distinctly well-worn. And today, 15 years later, the only fighter in service in the world that can definitely beat this performance is the Soviet MiG-25, which is a much later and less versatile aircraft built just for speed at high altitude.

On December 5, 1961 Cdr George W. Ellis, USN,

took off from Edwards to attempt the world record for sustained altitude. This demands judgement every bit as fine as precise navigation around a tricky desert racecourse, because to set the best figure it is necessary to select exactly the right conditions. The FAI rules decree that the contest aircraft may make one pass over the straight 15/25km course, and must neither decelerate nor descend more than 100m (328ft) between entry gate and exit. Obviously one sets full power on the engines, and here it was a matter for General Electric to check proper combustion in the engines and afterburners in the thin air. But if the pilot gets any of about ten major variables wrong, he will either set a poor figure or be disqualified. Basically, the lift of a wing depends on its angle to the airflow (angle of attack) and the square of the airspeed. The objective is to fly as fast as possible whilst setting the wing at the greatest angle of attack for maximum lift. But if one aims too high at the entry gate, loss of either height or speed during the run is inevitable, resulting in disqualification. Trying too hard would cause a stall, with no hope of trying again in that mission. With all the factors judged correctly the aircraft is flown straight and level, at high speed, yet close to the point of stalling all the way along the run.

Ellis climbed out to 40 000ft at a distance of 180 miles. Then he made a 180° turn and, a few minutes later, lit both burners and climbed at full power. Forty miles from the entry gate the Phantom had reached Mach 2·2 at 60 000ft. From that point Ellis climbed very carefully at constant calibrated airspeed to the height the computer said was correct for the record attempt. The subsequent analysis showed the entry gate was crossed at 66 443·8ft and the exit marker at 66 237·8ft. This complied with the rules, and as no speed had been lost Ellis had the record. The entry-gate figure beat the previous record by the enormous margin of more than 11 000ft, and has never been surpassed by a fighter (the YF-12A, which has flown higher, is a research aircraft).

The Phantom's spate of records was rounded off in early 1962 by Operation High Jump, a series of flights by different crews in which every existing time-to-height record was bettered by a wide margin. It is not possible just to open the throttles, take off and climb as fast as possible to the aircraft's ceiling, setting all the records on the way. Each flight has to be planned to reach a specific target height and to do so in minimum time by converting kinetic energy into altitude. On each flight the pilot had to follow a precise plan, which became more complex when aiming for upper levels.

The High Jump missions for 3, 6, 9, 12 and 15 thousand metres (9 843, 19 684, 29 528, 39 370 and 49 213ft) were all flown from NAS (Naval Air Station) Brunswick, Maine. First off was Lt-Cdr (later astronaut) John W. Young, USN. He opened up to full burner on the runway, with the flaps up, and the NAA timing official had to wave him away before the engines reached full thrust — which could make the Phantom tires slide round the locked wheels or along the runway. Young rotated and pulled off at the right moment, retracted the gear immediately, accelerated level to a predetermined speed and then pulled up at a planned rate of change of g and with a specified peak g until the prescribed climb angle was reached. All this happened in about 20sec, but it was done exactly according to plan. The climb angle was then held until the aircraft had passed the target flight level. The time for 3000m was 34·52sec, so that the Phantom was passing through the 10 000ft level 35sec after being stationary on the runway.

On the same day Cdr David M. Longton USN shot for 6 000m, using the same technique, returning a time of 48·78sec. On March 1, 1962 Lt-Col William C. McGraw Jr, USMC, thundered away to 9 000metres, clocking 61·62sec (an average rate of climb close to 30 000ft/min from a standing start), and then flew the 12 000m mission for a time of 77·15sec. The latter was the fastest mean rate of climb of all, equivalent to nearly 31 000 ft/min. At lower target heights too much time is taken in accelerating and getting into the climb; at greater heights, of course, the thin upper air cuts engine power and wing lift, and stretches out the in-flight time. But a third mission was flown on March 1, this time by Lt-Cdr Del W. Nordberg, USN. He set a time of 114·54sec to 15 000m.

The action then switched to NAS Point Mugu, California, where on March 31, Lt-Cdr F. Taylor Brown, USN, went for 20 000m. For this altitude, very close to the previously established maximum sustained level for the Phantom, a new technique was necessary. The aircraft had to be levelled off at a carefully selected intermediate level, accelerated at this height to a given Mach number, and again pulled up at a chosen g to a new climb angle to pass through the target height in minimum total time. Taylor went through 20 000m in 178·5sec. On April 3 Lt-Cdr Young, in a second mission, shot for 25 000m, a severe test needing a high supersonic acceleration at the intermediate level; his time was 230·4sec. Finally, on April 12, the top level of all was assigned to Nordberg. This demanded a maximum performance all the way, with well over Mach 2 at the intermediate level and a subsequent ballistic trajectory resembling the Top Flight mission of 1959. In the event, the time for 30 000m was 371·43sec, and the Phantom went on less than a second later to eclipse its Top Flight mark and finally go over the top at well over 100 000ft!

Even today, these figures are still dramatic and impressive. The Phantom just happened to be designed at the end of the 50-year period during which the flight speed and altitude capability of aircraft had increased year by year. Since then — say, 1958 — fighters have not got faster, nor reached out for greater height, with the exception of the very special-purpose MiG-25 'Foxbat' and the experimental Lockheed YF-12A. These much larger aircraft were built for speed, for research at high flight levels and Mach numbers and for reconnaissance over hostile territory. They cannot drop bombs or engage in a dogfight, and at low levels must not fly at full throttle or make any tight turns. Yet the Phantom can do all these things, and very much more. Coupled with its fantastic all-round flight performance, its versatility made it unquestionably the top fighter in the world from 1960 until 1975. Only now, in the final quarter of the century, have designers been able to produce even better fighters having later

engines, more advanced structures, newer radar and sighting systems, and other features which did not exist in the mid-1950s. Probably the best of all the new generation comes from the same design team and the same factory that built the Phantom   (p.60). Meanwhile, the Phantom itself has been considerably developed, to carry more loads further, climb even faster, pull more g in combat, and incorporate more versatile and effective armament.

Below: One of the first Marine Corps squadrons to be equipped with the F-4B was VMF(AW)-513, a crack outfit with a great record in World War II and Korea. This photograph was taken in 1962./*MCAIR*

Building the Phantom

Saint Louis was one of the pioneer settlements on the Mississippi in the vast American Midwest. It grew swiftly in the 19th century on a diet of cattle, railroads and an increasingly diverse manufacturing industry. Mr Mac arrived in an insignificant way in 1939, yet the company's technical boldness and skill pushed it up and up in the local hierarchy until in the 1950s it became the biggest employer in the entire Midwest. As the *St Louis Post-Dispatch* wrote in 1966, 'Anybody who gets caught in the traffic jam around Lambert-St Louis Field at 3·30pm, when shifts change, can tell without statistics how tall McDonnell stands in the St Louis economy.' Thanks to Mac, industrial employment has not fallen in the area over the past two decades, but instead has never ceased to rise. And over 80 per cent of the credit has been due to one product: the Phantom.

Like most other new aircraft, the Phantom at first accounted only for small local operations behind security screens in special departments, but by 1960 the big fighter had gone into production and swiftly filled most of the manufacturing floorspace. This happened just as the space age was getting into top gear — Sputnik I having been launched in October 1957 — and McDonnell gained the prime contract for both the first two generations of American manned spacecraft, the single-man Mercury and two-man Gemini. The company built a vast Space Center on the other side of Lambert civil airport from the aircraft plant, and the flawless succession of Mercury and Gemini flights in 1961-66 brought front-page fame around the world. But Mr Mac himself, James S.

Right: Home of the Phantom: Lambert-St Louis Airport, looking north-east, with runway 12/30 running right across the picture and the city and Mississippi river in the background. Phantom assembly takes place in building 1, left of centre. At extreme right is MDD Astronautics; company headquarters is off to the right./*MCAIR*

22

McDonnell, never doubted that in terms of hard cash the Phantom would be the most important of all the company's products during the lifetime of the programme. During the 1960s production grew at an accelerating rate, and, as the months went by, fate seemed ever to smile on the fighter from St Louis. It was designed for the Navy and Marine Corps, even though their admirals and generals had not asked for it. Flight trials against the F8U-3 resulted in its choice as an interceptor for both services. So outstanding did the Phantom prove that it was adopted as standard type by the US Air Force — an event without precedent. The Air Force developed it as a multi-role attack fighter and as a specialised multi-sensor reconnaissance aircraft, which in turn broadened the spectrum of roles and versions bought by the Navy and Marine Corps. The much-vaunted TFX swing-wing aircraft, planned by the Department of Defense to replace all earlier fighter and tactical attack aircraft for all the US services, did not succeed in this objective. The F-111B version for the Navy was abandoned, and the Air Force versions were bought in numbers much smaller than originally planned. Instead of being quickly phased out of production, the Phantom went from strength to strength. New versions for Britain swelled the line in the second half of the 1960s, and production never slackened. The only visible changes were that Phantoms were coming off the line in several different forms, and bearing the markings of an increasing number of customers. And new ones just kept on coming.

Right from the start the manufacturing programme was geared to a big long-run production schedule — evidence of faith in the qualities of the aircraft at a time when the number built might have been quite small. In typical US manner, the airframe was split into major assemblies which were subcontracted to other companies, so that Mac's actual manufacturing task was restricted to 45 per cent of the bare structure, or less than 20 per cent of the price of each aircraft. The rest of the airframe came from such companies as Fairchild-Republic, Cessna, Beech, Aeronca, Douglas, Northrop, Brunswick and Goodyear. Engines came from GE at Evendale (Cincinnati), and landing gears from Bendix. Mac's task was to unload the parts from the railroad cars and trucks, fix them all together, install the thousands of items of equipment and operating systems, check out the aircraft and test-fly it before delivery. Apart from the Japanese F-4EJ, every Phantom in the world has come off the line at St Louis, though the source of the parts has varied. German models have parts from MBB, Dornier and many other firms in West Germany; British ones incorporate parts from BAC, Short Brothers, Rolls-Royce and many other UK firms. These offsets helped home industry, and eased a balance-of-payments problem; but, like virtually all offsets, they increased the price, and in the case of the British aircraft seriously delayed delivery.

All the parts of each Phantom come together in Building 1 at St Louis, a vast flat box in typical American industrial style covering 15 acres or about

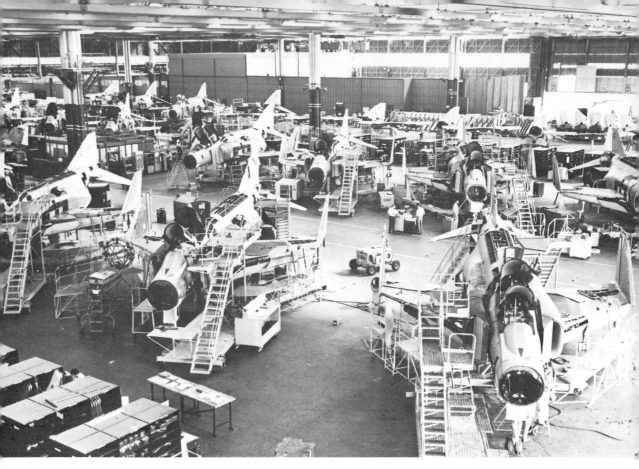

Above: Start of the flood: part of the final assembly line in 1963, when huge US Air Force orders were multiplying the already large backlog. At this time the only models in production were the B and C, and deliveries had not greatly exceeded 100./*MCAIR*

Left. Full spate: one of the final lines in December 1967. Nearest the camera is Phantom No 2 749, the 197th F-4J. Most of this line are Js, but the fourth aircraft along is the 792nd F-4D for the Air Force./*MCAIR*

Far left: Unfamiliar engine in the Mac factory! An American dolly rigged to instal the Rolls-Royce Spey 202/203 afterburning turbofan, destined for the YF-4K in the background. The engine and aircraft made their maiden flight together on June 27, 1966./*Rolls-Royce*

665 000 square feet. It is splendidly illuminated, with no hard shadows, and air-conditioned to keep the environment cool in the scorching Missouri summer, warm in the bitter winter and clean all the year round. The parallel final-assembly lines cover an area so great that from ground level the other side of the shop can hardly be seen. Everywhere is bustle and colour, yet the background noise level is low. The rattles and whines of a thousand rivet guns, drills and countless other compressed-air tools, the rustle of complex parts being withdrawn from their packaging, and the soft voices of the scattered humans — whites and blacks, men and women — all hustling to build the Phantom add up to a murmur like the sea on a distant shore.

Left: The man who represents the customer at St Louis is the NavPlantRep, head of a large office that oversees every detail of every F-4. Here, on a misty morning in March 1967, Capt John C Kane Jr gets the signatures of the Air Force crew collecting a rather special F-4D./*MCAIR*

Below: A McDonnell Douglas test Phantom, not exactly representative of any production version. This example has nose pitot/yawmeter probe, RF-type nose, experimental wing slats (hence the 'Project Agile Eagle' crest on the inlet), EROS (Eliminate Range-zero System) collision-avoidance payload, and an experimental beryllium rudder./*MCAIR*

Below right: A newly completed F-4F at St Louis, incorporating a substantial proportion of German airframe parts and equipment items./*MCAIR*

The floor is spotless and everywhere exactly level, though one must watch out for air lines, electric cables, and special test equipment.

Major chunks of Phantom gleam with polished aluminium, reflect the light from brightly coloured protective coatings, or have the dull appearance of titanium or glass fibre. No previous fighter had more titanium, which accounts for 7·7 per cent of an F-4B, 8·5 per cent of an E or J, and 9·4 per cent of a K or M. No previous fighter had so much integrally-machined primary structure, or so much that was chem-milled. The big pieces of airframe come from all over the United States or from Europe, and reach the line fully equipped and wired with the Phantom's braided compact wire bundles, which save space and weight and by being completely potted and sealed avoid moisture problems. Multi-pin plugs were from the start provided with several spare pigtails for extra circuits which became needed in later versions with more equipment. The most complex part of the whole aircraft is the nose, and this is made in left and right halves so that each side can be virtually finished. When they are joined there is room for only one man in each cockpit, and he has the barest minimum of final connecting-up to do. Finally all the sections run together, on bright yellow dollies, and the Phantom rapidly takes shape under the skilled hands that have done it anything up to 5 000 times before.

At the end of the line the whole ship has come together, with all the right parts to make a gunned and slatted E, or a multi-sensor RF, or a rebuilt S for the Navy. It goes to the paint shop, where 28½ gallons of epoxy camouflage paint is sprayed on, topped by national markings that will resist a thousand super-sonic rainstorms, a thousand hours in the high stratosphere, and a thousand takeoffs over the desert or a salty carrier deck.

Altogether, the Phantom manufacturing operation is a model of the way it ought to be. Most types of air-craft are built only in small numbers. They never get far down the learning curve — the curve of manufac-turing man-hours and cost plotted against the number built, which reflects the fact that, the more of one type you can build, the faster and cheaper you can do it. Of course in a world of severe inflation it is very hard to make things progressively cheaper, but in the case of the Phantom it brought down the price for years and even today enables Mac to turn out a Phantom at a very competitive price that is still lower than the unit cost of the first batch. Most of the Phantoms have gone out of the door with a price tag of about $1·7million, including everything but the ordnance (guns, ammunition, missiles and bombs). Today the bare airframe runs close to $1·5million, with the engines, systems and equipment costing rather more, to push the price over the $3million mark. On the other hand, today's Phantom is a considerably better aircraft; nothing else with comparable hitting power and all-weather multi-mission capability can be had for less than three times the price.

In late 1976 the 5 000th Phantom was about to go out of the door. Elsewhere in Building 1 is the growing line where they assemble the later, fractionally bigger, totally different, and far more costly F-15 Eagle. But the Phantom has one of the key qualities of truly great aircraft. Customers have kept on asking for more, and the end of the line — even of new builds — is still some way off.

Phantom Variants

Almost every good aircraft in history has had the potential for extensive development. Put another way, none has ever been so perfect that it could not be bettered. In the case of the Phantom, it has been mainly internal engineering development that has lifted this fighter out of the confines of a single customer and turned it into a tremendous world-wide success serving many customers in many roles. Its massive, cranky shape has never significantly altered, and the engine power has not grown to anything like the degree seen in the Spitfire or Sabre; but the detail aerodynamic design, the systems engineering, and the equipment fit, have all been grossly altered and updated, partly to incorporate the lessons of combat experience, and partly to take in the benefits of later technology. Even today the process is continuing, and to write the definitive story of the Phantom would mean waiting until the next century.

F-4A Originally there were to have been 23 pre-production aircraft (including the two prototypes) and 24 production machines, all incorporated in the December 1958 contract when the two XF4H-1s were already flying. Actually, though 47 aircraft were indeed built as F-4As, the first 26 were used as R&D (research and development) vehicles while the final 21 were assigned to training squadrons. Even then the precise standard of build kept changing — as is almost always the case at such an early stage — and during the 1960s most of the surviving A models were brought up almost to F-4B standard. In the first 18 aircraft the top line of the canopy was flush with the top of the fuselage, for minimum supersonic drag. Again in these first 18, the radar originally fitted was the APQ-50 Mod, with 24in dish aerial (antenna); later As had the bigger APQ-72, but this is officially

Right: Always flamboyant exponents of the Phantom, VF-84, from *Independence*, wear the Jolly Roger on their tails./*MCAIR*

regarded as an F-4B change. The engine was the J79-2, rated at 10 350lb dry (military) thrust, with 16 150lb available with afterburner. The F-4A was first delivered to a special Navy unit, VF-101, for conversion training and carrier qualification trials in December 1960. This was 2½ years after first flight.

TF-4A Designation of surviving A models still used in various training roles, without being converted to B standard.

F-4B The original bulk-production version for the US Navy and Marine Corps inventory. Engines were the more powerful, and much more fully equipped, J79-8, rated at 10 900lb military power and 17 000lb with afterburner. These engines, with airflow increased from 166 to 170 lb/sec, were fed by slightly enlarged inlets with a changed ramp actuation geometry (fixed ramp 10° instead of 5°, variable ramp 14° instead of 10°) for improved performance. Following carrier trials crew vision was improved by raising the level of the seats to give both pilot and RIO (radar intercept officer) better view ahead, necessitating a higher canopy. The radar was changed to the APQ-72, whose 32in dish caused a marked bulging of the nose, which was also pointed downwards (giving a double-curve to the bottom profile) to improve pilot view on carrier approach. Internal fuel capacity was standardised at 1 665gal (2 000 USgal) in six fuselage bladders and integral tanks formed by sealing each

Above: A beautifully judged arrival aboard *Independence* by a VF-84 F-4B, with centreline tank and Sidewinders. In the foreground, an A-4 and the tail of a VF-41 Phantom./*USN*

Right: Quarterdeck of USS *Enterprise* (CVAN-65), at the time (1962) the world's largest ship and indisputably the most expensive. The F-4Bs belong to VF-103./*MCAIR*

wing box between the fold lines. In a flush compartment on the right of the cockpits is a long hinged flight-refuelling probe. Main landing gears, which like all Phantom gears are Bendix products, are of ultra-high-tensile 140ton steel, stressed to allow recovery at a sink rate of 24 feet per second at a weight of 34 000lb. Other electronic equipment includes a General Electric ASA-32 autopilot, Lear AJB-3 bombing system, Eclipse-Pioneer dead-reckoning navigation computer, AiResearch air-data computer, Raytheon radio altimeter and ACF infra-red (IR) detector in a large fairing under the radome. To help fly through hostile airspace most B models have the Magnavox APR-27 surface/air missile launch warning receiver, and of course various ECM pods can be carried externally. Standard armament comprises four

Sparrow radar-homing air/air missiles recessed into the underside of the fuselage and two more Sparrows, or four close-range Sidewinders, on the inboard wing pylons. In a surface attack role the B could carry up to 16 000lb of ordnance including every airborne store at present deployed aboard US Navy carriers (the A-3 Skywarrior H-bomb is no longer used) and every airborne store of the Marine Corps. McDonnell built 637 B models, not including F-4A conversions nor the 12 F-4Gs.

DF-4B Designation of small number of B models modified as 'mother aircraft' to RPVs and drones.

QF-4B This is the designation of the F-4B rebuilt as an RPV (remotely-piloted vehicle) by the Naval Air Development Center, Warminster, Pennsylvania. One of the largest and most powerful RPVs yet flown, the QF-4B is normally flown with a safety pilot on board, though under the direct control of a remote pilot in another aircraft (often a DF-4B) or on the ground. Their assignments have included basic research, air-/ground weapon trials, ACM (air-combat manoeuvring), air/air weapon trials, and ECM-aided penetration of simulated heavily defended airspace. The first QF flew in late 1971, and at least 44 had been converted at NADC by 1975.

Above: The QF-4B is an RPV (remotely piloted vehicle) used by the US Navy Missile Center at Pt Mugu, usually in connection with the development of new air-combat missiles. There were 44 such converted Phantoms, often flown by pilots in DF-8L Crusaders many miles distant./*USN*

Above right: The first RF-4B for the Marine Corps, parked shiny and new in June 1966 next to a heavily laden F-4D of the Air Force. The RF-4B has the basic airframe of the B, but with inertial navigation and mission equipment generally similar to the RF-4C./ *MCAIR*

RF-4B No reconnaissance version of the Phantom was at first planned by the Navy, but when the Air Force developed the RF-4C a batch of 12 aircraft was bought for the Marine Corps designated RF-4B. These essentially package the reconnaissance systems of the RF-4C, with inertial navigation, into the basic air-

frame of the F-4B. The ALR 17 ELRAC is not fitted, and the forward and side oblique cameras have rotatable mounts. Altogether 46 were delivered, all of them F-4B conversions for the Marines. First flight March 1965.

F-4C In 1961 the Department of Defense, despite its fixation on the TFX project, was so impressed by the Phantom it ordered a series of direct competitive evaluations against US Air Force aircraft. The result was the discovery that the F-4B had better radar than the best land-based interceptor, carried a bigger load further than the best Air Force attack aircraft, and was potentially the world's best tactical reconnaissance aircraft. It also demonstrated better serviceability and lower maintenance man-hours per flight hour than any USAF 'Century series' fighter (the best of which in this regard was Mac's own F-101). The result was that in March 1962 the Phantom was adopted as the primary weapon system of USAF Tactical Air Command — the first time a Navy aircraft had ever been adopted as a major combat type for the Air Force. At first designated F-110A, it was restyled F-4C in the new standardised Department of Defense numbering system introduced in 1962. On the whole the big Phantom represented a quantum jump in tactical-aircraft capability, despite being compromised by a rigorously imposed policy of minimal change from the Navy F-4B. The folding wings and deck hook were retained, and engineering changes were restricted to those the Air Force deemed essential. One alteration was to use the J79-15 engine, with a self-contained cartridge/pneumatic starter on the lower wheelcase instead of the Navy turbine-impingement method that required an externally coupled air hose. The 20 kVA alternator on each engine was moved from the waist gearbox to the bullet fairing on the nose. The FR probe was replaced by a KC-135 boom receptacle on top of the mid-fuselage. The main wheels and tyres of the F-4B, 30in by 7·7in, were too small and hard for tactical airfields, and were widened to 11·5in. This allowed the brakes to be made more powerful, augmented by an added anti-skid system, but it also meant shallow bulges in the wing roots to accommodate the retracted wheels. More complete dual controls were fitted; at first a TAC Phantom crew comprised two rated pilots, the front-seater being the AC (aircraft commander) and the back-seater the pilot, but in 1970 the back-seater increasingly became the WSO (weapon-system operator), not necessarily pilot-rated. The rear-cockpit instrument panel was lowered to improve forward view (odd that the Navy never did this) and there were various instrument changes. The radar was modified into the APQ-100,

Far left top: The first F-4s to join the Air Force were actually a pair of Navy F-4Bs, with BuAer Nos 149405-6, lent to Tactical Air Command for evaluation and initial crew training. Here they are engaged in stores trials, wearing TAC badges and with the bastardised serial numbers '64-9405' and '64-9406'. A little later, on November 20, 1963, a ceremony at MacDill AFB (Tampa, Florida) marked formal introduction of the F-4C to service. By this time the command had many Navy Bs and true production Cs./*USAF*

Far left bottom: Scene at MacDill in April 1964. Thirty ex-Navy F-4Bs and true TAC F-4Cs are visible. This was a time when training of Air Force air and ground crews on the F-4 was a priority task./*MCAIR*

Above: Exercise Winter Trail in 1963-4 was the first major overseas deployment of the Air Force F-4C. Here two of the new aircraft (63-7537 and 7561) are seen at 'forty below' at Orland Air Base, Norway, after a refuelled Arctic flight./*RNorAF*

Centre left: Ground crew wave out a C-12 from the flight-line of the 121st Sqn, Ejercito del Aire (Spanish Air Force). The C-12 is the F-4C, used in both defence and tactical roles. Officer commanding 121 is Lt-Col Delgado Arjona./*Howard Levy*

Below left: A C-12 of the 122nd Sqn (aircraft 122-04). Commanded by Lt-Col Gabaldon, this unit received 18 Phantoms, as did 121. Both squadrons form the 12th Air Defence Wing, based at Torrejon together with three ageing KC-97L tankers of 123 Tanker Sqn./*Howard Levy*

with a new rear-cockpit scope giving a better mapping display. An important change was replacement of the nav computer by the Litton ASN-48 inertial system. An AJB-7 bombing system and LADD timer were added, together with pylon provisions for the GAM-83B Bullpup air/ground missile and the associated command guidance box in the rear cockpit. The first C flew on May 27, 1963 and the 583rd and last was delivered in May 1966. Standard equipment in TAC, PACAF (Pacific Air Forces) and USAFE (USAF Europe). Some have been passed on to other air forces, including 36 (known as C-12s) to Spain.

RF-4C Intended as a replacement for the McDonnell RF-101C, this unarmed tactical reconnaissance version soon became the standard USAF aircraft in this category. It was an ideal fit of a comprehensive array of optical, radar and IR sensors into the basic USAF F-4 airframe, with dual controls, giving a radius of action of the order of 1 000miles, in all weathers. Removal of the missiles and recesses, radar and all armament fire-control enabled more than 40 new items to be installed. The new nose, 33in longer and of more

tapering form, contains a small APQ-99 forward-looking radar with mapping, terrain-following and terrain-avoidance modes. Immediately behind it is the camera bay, which can be configured for low-altitude day, low-altitude night or high-altitude day missions. There is invariably a forward oblique camera, a panoramic camera giving 180° low or (with gyro-stabilisation) 90° high lateral coverage, or various arrangements of triples, split verticals or framing cameras. For fast low photography precise image-motion compensation is provided to eliminate blurring. Below the forward fuselage is an APQ-102 side-looking aircraft radar (SLAR) to give a high-definition film radar picture along each side of the flight path. Just behind it is an AAS-118 IR reconnaissance system (IRRS) giving a linescan picture of temperature variation of surface targets, by day or night. IR linescan can reveal the presence of humans, show where a truck was recently parked, which aircraft of a line-up has just run its engines or even which has lately been refuelled. Most RF-4Cs also bristle with mission electronics. A near-standard fitment is the Electronic Specialty ALR-17 ELRAC, tied in with

Left: McDonnell flight test crew — Jack Krings, pilot, and B A McIntyre, observer — climb aboard the first RF-4C reconnaissance Phantom for familiarisation prior to the maiden flight on May 18, 1964. The previous year two converted Navy F-4Bs had flown as YRF-4Cs with mock-ups of the new nose./*MCAIR*

Top: An RF-4C (66-0438) of the 432nd TRW at about 1 000ft over SE Asia in December 1967. The Tac Recon Wings operated in this theatre by day and night, in all weathers, getting photo, IR and radar coverage of remarkably difficult targets./*USAF*

Above: External inspection of a parked RF-4C, in the pre-camouflage days when the finish was pale pearly grey The HF shunt aerial along the front of the fin stands out clearly./*USAF*

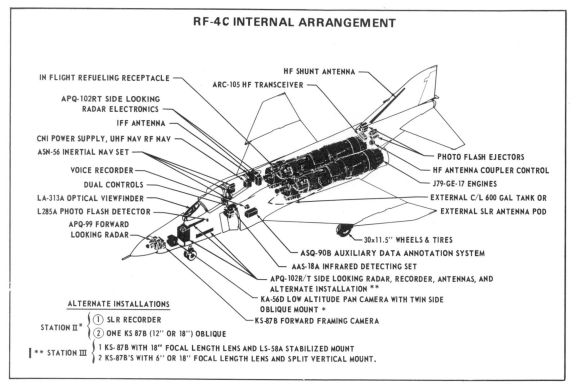

RF-4C INTERNAL ARRANGEMENT

IN FLIGHT REFUELING RECEPTACLE

HF SHUNT ANTENNA
ARC-105 HF TRANSCEIVER

APQ-102RT SIDE LOOKING
RADAR ELECTRONICS

IFF ANTENNA

CNI POWER SUPPLY, UHF NAV RF NAV

ASN-56 INERTIAL NAV SET

VOICE RECORDER

DUAL CONTROLS

LA-313A OPTICAL VIEWFINDER

L285A PHOTO FLASH DETECTOR

APQ-99 FORWARD
LOOKING RADAR

PHOTO FLASH EJECTORS

HF ANTENNA COUPLER CONTROL

J79-GE-17 ENGINES

EXTERNAL C/L 600 GAL TANK OR

EXTERNAL SLR ANTENNA POD

30x11.5" WHEELS & TIRES

ASQ-90B AUXILIARY DATA ANNOTATION SYSTEM

AAS-18A INFRARED DETECTING SET

APQ-102R/T SIDE LOOKING RADAR, RECORDER, ANTENNAS, AND
ALTERNATE INSTALLATION **

KA-56D LOW ALTITUDE PAN CAMERA WITH TWIN SIDE
OBLIQUE MOUNT *

KS-87B FORWARD FRAMING CAMERA

ALTERNATE INSTALLATIONS

STATION II* { ① SLR RECORDER
② ONE KS 87B (12" OR 18") OBLIQUE

** STATION III { 1 KS-87B WITH 18" FOCAL LENGTH LENS AND LS-58A STABILIZED MOUNT
2 KS-87B'S WITH 6" OR 18" FOCAL LENGTH LENS AND SPLIT VERTICAL MOUNT.

the cameras for automatic identification and classification of hostile radars on photo maps. A far bigger equipment, carried in lieu of a tank on the centreline pylon, is the AIL ALQ-61 ELINT (electronic intelligence) airborne receiver and recording system. Itek's APR-25 crystal video receiver is usually fitted to give a coarse bearing of hostile threats, and this is generally associated with the APR-26 missile-launch warning receiver. A near-standard Westinghouse pod is the ALQ-101 combined noise and repeater jammer, and there are now several later ECM and ELINT devices aboard RF Phantoms. The inertial system is the ASN-56. In the rear fuselage is a large 'photo cart' array, which upon command ejects flash cartridges vertically upwards. Near it is the powerful HF single-sideband (SSB) radio, ARC-105, for instant contact with ground bases out to the limit of range, where UHF (with line-of-sight limitation) would be useless. This was the first supersonic aircraft to have HF radio, and the entire fin leading edge serves as the shunt aerial. In most configurations some cameras, such as low panoramic installations, can process their film in flight and eject the developed cassette in a protective capsule over a ground command post before returning to base. Engines are J79-15, and the tyres are 11·5in wide. First flight May 1964: the 505th and last was delivered in December 1973.

F-4D In March 1964 the Air Force obtained authority to go ahead on this version tailored more closely to its needs, using the F-4C airframe but with a greatly updated equipment fit. The radar is the partly solid-state APQ-109, which is smaller and lighter and provides an air/ground ranging capability with movable cursors. A completely new servoed sight, the ASG-22 LCOSS (lead-computing optical sight system), is fitted, together with associated lead-computing gyro and amplifier. These items are mounted in No 1 tank bay, along with the ASQ-91 weapon release computer, and the bay was given a cooling-air duct. Immediately ahead of these racks is the improved ASG-63 inertial navigation system (INS). The result is an aircraft with considerably enhanced accuracy in attack on surface targets, with reduced crew-workload, partly as a result of widespread automaticity instead of the mainly manual systems of the Navy Phantom. To supply the greater electrical power the alternators are uprated to 30 kVA, and provision is made for an ever wider spectrum of external ordnance and electronic payloads. The D model is compatible with the Maverick air-/ground missile and Falcon air/air missile, and with all USAF 'smart' (laser-guided) bombs, as described later. Standard equipment includes the Bendix APS-107 radar homing and warning system and Itek APR-36 radar warning receiver (an improved APR-25).

Top left: For the buffs who enjoy reams of technical hardware, this sketch gives an idea of the amount of mission equipment built into the basic RF-4C. ECM and other devices can be fixed on outside.

Above: Together with the F-5E Tiger II, the only effective aircraft of the Republic of Korea Air Force comprise 18 F-4C and 18 F-4D Phantoms, one of the latter being pictured. Confronting them in North Korea are more than 500 MiGs./*MCAIR*

Centre left: Against a background of British 'clag' two C-models from the 48th TFW climb steadily carrying tanks, mission electronics and centreline gun pods./*USAFE*

Below left: Scramble from the runway at RAF Mildenhall, Suffolk, home of the 48th TFW. All Phantoms in USAF Europe are camouflaged./*USAFE*

Many jamming and chaff (Window) pods can be fitted, and altogether the F-4D marks a major advance over the B and C. First flown in December 1965, the D was at one time the most numerous type of Phantom, and it was the mainstay of the USAF in Vietnam. Total production was 843, of which 32 were supplied to the Imperial Iranian Air Force and 18, from USAF stocks, to the Republic of Korea AF.

F-4E This US Air Force model was planned to be similar to the D apart from having a major change in radar and weapon-control system. The planned radar was to be either the pulse-doppler APG-59 or APQ-109/CORDS, while the missile-control system was to be the Aero-1A, as in previous models, or the new AWG-10. In the event Westinghouse produced a completely new all-solid-state radar, the APQ-120, which

Left: The internal gun of the F-4E was entirely welcome. Here taking a look at the first E to join the Air Force are (right) Col Floyd White of the 4525th Fighter Weapons Wing at Nellis (whence he had just flown the aircraft from Mac's plant) and Maj Everett T. Raspberry, wing project officer for the E. The date was October 3, 1967. Earlier that year Raspberry had shot down a MiG-21 and MiG-17./*USAF*

Top: For self-evident reasons the Heyl Ha'Avir (Israel Defence Force/Air Force) is coy about discussing its Phantoms or anything else. But this machine is one of about 204 F-4Es, a trickle of which are still being supplied new to replace second-hand ex-USAF aircraft./*Israeli Official*

Above: Mission completed, an Israeli F-4E of an unmentionable unit returns to its base somewhere in Israel (perhaps even that is an unjustified assumption!)./*Israeli Official*

is significantly lighter, more compact and more reliable than previous Phantom radars. The reduced size of dish (elliptical, 27·5in × 24·5in), which still scans mechanically, shows the change in wavelength and needs a considerably smaller radome. While the E was still in the works the perhaps belated decision was taken to fit an internal gun, and as described later this was fitted in the underside of the considerably lengthened nose, with 640-round ammunition tank immediately behind. The IR seeker is no longer fitted. To preserve balance it was found possible to add a new fuselage fuel cell, No 7, above the engine nozzles and under the fin. This extra weight at both ends of the longer fuselage was countered by fitting the J79-17 engine, with afterburning thrust of 17 900lb. The seats are 'zero-zero' Martin-Baker rocket-assisted, cleared for use at zero altitude and zero airspeed. The slotted stabilator (tailplane) of the J, K and M is fitted. The first F-4E flew in June 1967 and was delivered for USAF testing in October of that year. From June

Top: A rare display of Israeli aviation hardware, included in which was one of the new 'post-war' E-model Phantoms and all Phantom stores (including the M61 gun and its ammunition). Israel Aircaft Industries has been striving for increased self-sufficiency, especially in electronics and ordnance, and makes the Shafrir AAM./*Israeli Official*

Above: One of the F-4Es leased by the RAAF from the US Government in 1970 is pictured before delivery. The Australians hired 24 Phantoms at Amberley, Queensland, to tide them over until, ten years after placing an order for F-111Cs, they finally took delivery of the problem-ridden swing-winger. One F-4E crashed and the rest were returned in 1973./*MCAIR*

1972, when several hundred E models had been delivered, the decision was taken to fit the slatted wing which, as described on page 68, had been studied by Mac for years and had previously been specified for the F-4EF. Slats have subsequently been retrofitted on virtually every F-4E previously delivered, with TISEO (page 96) on the fixed inboard leading edge (USAF only). The E has also become the main export model, usually without certain items of classified equipment but sometimes including special national features. Among the recipients are Israel (about 200 F-4D, F-4E and RF-4E), Greece (38), Turkey (40), Iran (219), and Spain (18). In 1970-73 the RAAF leased 24 from the US Government as a stop-gap pending delivery of the same number of F-111Cs. This is by far the most important current model of Phantom, and about 2 000 had been delivered by 1976.

F-4EF Redesignated F-4F.

F-4EJ This is the only type of Phantom assembled away from St Louis, though many plants in several countries have made major components. The customer is the Japan Air Self-Defence Force, and the EJ differs in equipment fit from the basic E. USAF rear-warning radar not being available, a Japanese

Below: An EJ of 302 Sqn, JASDF, based at Chitose AB, Hokkaido, taxies out at Misawa AB on May 25, 1975. At this time the JASDF had received 85 Japanese-built Phantoms, as well as 14 RF-4EJ reconnaissance versions delivered from St Louis./*Mitsubishi*

Bottom: Arrival in Japan of the first F-4EJ, one of two previously assembled and tested at St Louis. This aircraft later took its place in the Japanese Air Self-Defence Force./*Takahashi*

counterpart is (or will be) fitted, and the intention is to make the aircraft compatible with the Mitsubishi AAM-2 collision-course air/air missile, with Nippon Electric IR homing head, though this is not yet close to service use. By the time this book is published all 128 EJs ought to be in service. The first two were delivered from St Louis in July 1971, the next eight were assembled by Mitsubishi at Nagoya, and the remainder have been built by Mitsubishi in partnership with Kawasaki and other Japanese companies.

EF-4E During the Vietnam conflict many F-105G Thunderchief attack aircraft were rebuilt as Wild Weasel ECM (electronic countermeasures) carriers for the suppression of hostile defences, especially SAMs (surface-to-air missiles). The successor, in the Advanced Wild Weasel programme, is the EF-4E Phantom. Study of specialised ECM versions of the F-4 began in 1968; two F-4Ds were evaluated with original Wild Weasel equipment, which included Westinghouse ECM pods and mixes of Shrike and Standard ARM missiles, and by 1974 the USAF had two squadrons of EF-4Cs. The EF-4E is a much bigger rebuild, with the major APR-38 system comprising a torpedo-like pod on the fin, plus further aerials, and an exceptional array of 'black boxes' in the fuselage, some occupying the bay formerly used for the gun, with control and display systems in both cockpits. The EF-4E could operate as a self-contained hunter-killer, but will normally serve as part of a larger attacking force. A total of 116, all conversions of existing E models, is planned to be completed by 1980.

RF-4E This multi-sensor reconnaissance aircraft combines the nose and basic mission equipment of the RF-4C with the airframe and engines of the E. Many of the classified US equipments are not fitted, because all

Above right: Thumbs up, having made certain that the hydraulically driven canopy is locked./*German Official*

Below right: A pair of RF-4Es of the Luftwaffe taxying out with three fuel pods and some ECM./*German Official*

Below: The Luftwaffe has two geschwader (wings) of RF-4E reconnaissance Phantoms, AG 51 at Bremgarten and AG 52 at Leck, with 30 aircraft each. Here an AG 51 pilot gets aboard./*German Official*

of this variant so far built have been for export customers. In-flight rotatable camera mounts are fitted, as in the RF-4Bs. Usually the SLAR is an advanced Goodyear installation, there is a varying fit of penaids (penetration aids — electronic-warfare and similar devices) and in Luftwaffe service, at least, there is a broadband air/ground digital data-link for all kinds of reconnaissance information including pictures. No internal gun is fitted, and flight refuelling is usually not provided for. The original customer was the West German Luftwaffe. When the agreement to buy 88 of this new model was signed in 1968 the Germans gained a potentially valuable offset in that their aircraft firms could bid on $125million of selected F-4 work in 1969-74 (all on batches subsequent to the RF-4E deliveries). US companies, with almost 4 000 Phantoms behind them, considered this 'mere window-dressing'; but, to their surprise, German companies proved to be able to underbid them on many hundreds of ship-sets of major airframe parts for all Phantoms — not just those for the Luftwaffe — MBB alone gaining orders worth over $25 million. This opened the way to a further major share in the German F-4F programme. Other users include Israel (see F-4E for total number), Iran (10) and Japan (14, delivered from St Louis).

Above: An unusual view of four Luftwaffe RF-4Es in echelon. Normally, an RF would work singly, and at a considerably lower or higher level than this./*German Official*

Above right: Two F-4F Phantoms of JG74 "Molders" based at Neuburg seen at low level over southern Germany in formation with a USAF F-4D Phantom from the 52nd TFW at Spangdahlem./*USAFE*

Right: Returning from a training mission, this F-4F wears the badge of the famed "Richthofen" Geschwader./*German Official*

F-4F In the late 1960s the Luftwaffe, which had been looking for a new air-superiority fighter, eventually decided on a new version of the Phantom. Designated F-4EF, this differed from all other variants in being a single-seater, and it was born as a competitor in the

US International Fighter Competition of 1969-71. It was to have the internal gun, slats, simplified APQ-120 radar, only six fuselage fuel cells, no flight refuelling, and a generally lightened and simplified structure and equipment. External weapon loads were greatly reduced, the normal maximum being centreline tank and four Sidewinders. Eventually the plan was changed, undoubtedly wisely, and the resulting order was for the F-4F which is closely similar to the two-seat F-4E. It differs mainly in electronic equipment and systems, partly because the US devices are classified and not available for export and partly to meet the specialised needs of the Luftwaffe or German industry. Unlike the E it has no No 7 tank, no provision for Sparrows, unslotted tailplane and neither TISEO nor surface-attack systems. Total 175, costing over $750 million, with outer wings, aft fuselage, tail and many equipment items, as well as the engines, shipped from Germany for assembly at St Louis. First flight, May 1973; deliveries, June 1973 to April 1976.

F-4G Designation of 12 aircraft modified during the production run of the F-4B to incorporate an ASW-21 two-way digital data link. To provide racking space the No 1 fuselage fuel cell was reduced in size and a new equipment compartment added between it and the rear cockpit, with access through a dorsal door. This No 1 tank equipment compartment proved invaluable and was later made standard on the F-4D, E and J. An additional equipment in the G was an approach power compensation system for use in a new automatic carrier landing mode. The G was first flown in March 1963 and used for extensive Navy data-link development. In 1966 some served over Vietnam with VF-213

aboard USS *Kitty Hawk*. Later these aircraft were restored to F-4B configuration. The ASW-21 and approach-power compensator were made standard in the F-4J.

F-4H Not used, because of confusion with original designation F4H.

F-4J Having carefully studied the changes between their own F-4B and the Air Force F-4C the Navy drew up a specification in 1963 for an F-4B follow-on making the best compromise between available hardware, new developments and mission performance. Emphasis was placed on the CAP fighter role though the F-4J is also used by the Marine Corps. The J model was planned in parallel with the F-4D, but is in many respects a more advanced aircraft because the

Top right: Sunset over solid British "clag" adds colour to a Phantom FG.1 of 892 Sqn, Royal Navy./*MoD official*

Bottom right: Flame, cases and gun-gas spew from the "Gatling" pod of an FGR.2 on a firing run over an offshore target./*MoD official*

Below: Front end of USS *Saratoga* (CVA-60) in 1969, showing an F-4J of VF-103 and Phantom FG.1 of 892 Sqn RN about to be launched. The different angle of the British aircraft, with extra-extended nose gear, is apparent. Behind it is the F-4J of VF-31 that three years later was to shoot down a MiG-21 in the hands of Cdr Sam Flynn./*USN*

need to make a heavier aircraft compatible with carrier operation resulted in significant airframe changes. Most important change in the J is not externally evident. As described in a later chapter, Westinghouse could by the early 1960s offer a radar of the fundamentally new pulse-doppler type, and one of these, the APG-59, was chosen for the F-4J. It was incorporated into a new integrated missile control system designated AWG-10, which was later made partly digital as the AWG-10(A). The APG-59 radar fits in a nose similar to the F-4B, while the AWG-10 fire control and computer units go in No 1 tank compartment together with the ASW-25 one-way digital data link. The IR seeker is not fitted. The bombing system is the AJB-7, the CNI (communications/navigation/IFF — identification friend or foe) is miniaturised solid-state, the pilot has the VTAS helmet sight and GVR-10 vertical gyro, there is a completely new equipment-cooling package (later also fitted to the F-4E), and a completely new fit of electronic-warfare equipment is provided including APR-32 homing and warning, with large fin-cap aerial, and the ALE-35 pyrotechnic dispenser. In the rear fuselage is the No 7 fuel tank. To handle the increased weight the engines are J79-10s, rated at 17 900lb and at Mach 2 at 36 000ft each giving more than 2 000lb greater thrust than an F-4B engine. They have automatic approach power compensators. The seats are Martin-Baker rocket-assisted, with zero-height, zero-airspeed capability. To make the J compatible with carrier operation the inboard leading edge is fixed, the ailerons are arranged to droop 16½° with gear down and the tailplane incorporates a fixed inverted slot along the leading edge; these changes actually reduce the approach speed, typically from 137 to 125 knots. The main gears are restressed for recovery at 38 000lb, at 23·3ft per second sink rate, and the tyres are the 30 × 11·5in pattern previously chosen by the Air Force. Finally, to meet the demands of increased electrical load with

Left: A bolter: having been waved-off back there in the smoke, an F-4J (unit unidentified) overshoots on both engines in March 1967. Another is stropped up on No 3 catapult, while spotted behind are two Douglas products, an A-4E and RA-3B./*MCAIR*

Below left: Friendly box formed by three J-models of VF-103 (*Saratoga*) and an FG.1 of 892 Sqn RN./*USN*

Below: Formation lift-off by three of the 'Blue Angels', the premier Navy aerobatic display team. Resplendent in deep blue and gold, the aircraft are J-models, on this occasion with a full kit of dummy Sparrows./*USN*

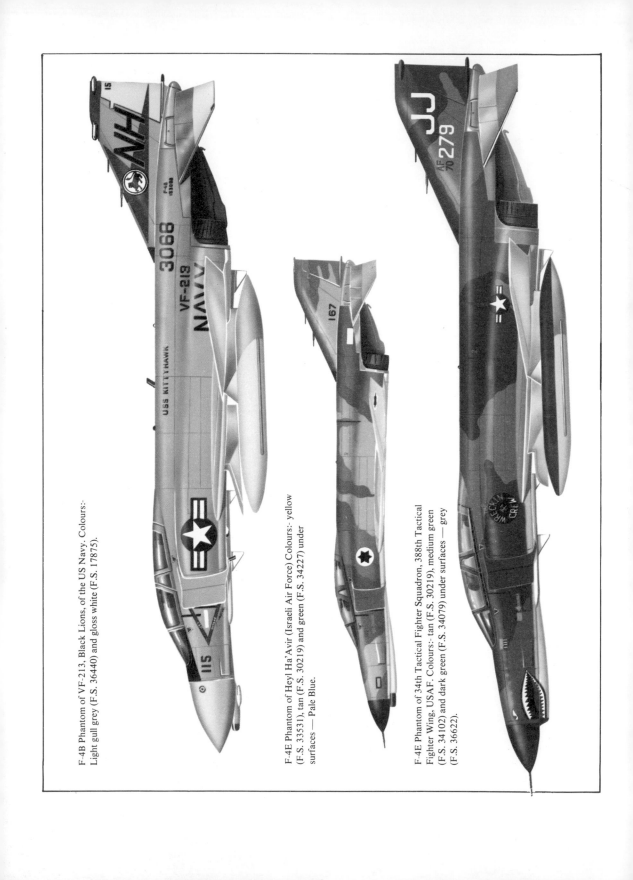

F-4B Phantom of VF-213, Black Lions, of the US Navy. Colours:- Light gull grey (F.S. 36440) and gloss white (F.S. 17875).

F-4E Phantom of Heyl Ha'Avir (Israeli Air Force) Colours:- yellow (F.S. 33531), tan (F.S. 30219) and green (F.S. 34227) under surfaces — Pale Blue.

F-4E Phantom of 34th Tactical Fighter Squadron, 388th Tactical Fighter Wing, USAF. Colours:- tan (F.S. 30219), medium green (F.S. 34102) and dark green (F.S. 34079) under surfaces — grey (F.S. 36622).

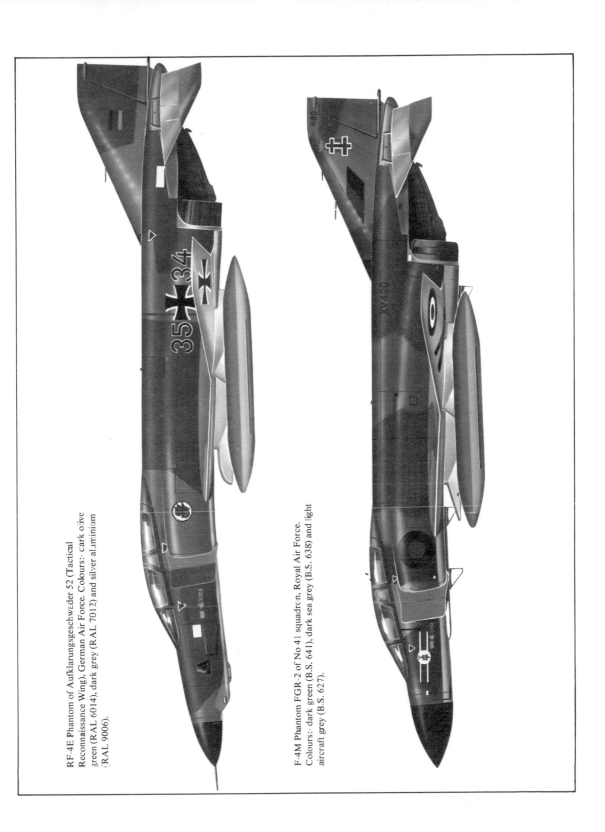

RF-4E Phantom of Aufklarungsgeschwader 52 (Tactical Reconnaissance Wing), German Air Force. Colours:- dark olive green (RAL 6014), dark grey (RAL 7012) and silver aluminium (RAL 9006).

F-4M Phantom FGR-2 of No 41 squadron, Royal Air Force. Colours:- dark green (B.S. 641), dark sea grey (B.S. 638) and light aircraft grey (B.S. 627).

precise frequency, the alternators are 30 kVA, mounted on constant-speed drives. First flight was in June 1966, and the 522nd and last was delivered in December 1972.

F-4J (AC) US Marine Corps F-4J Air Combat version, with digital AWG-10(A) and slatted wing.

F-4K When the Royal Navy decided in February 1964 to abandon the P.1154RN and buy the Phantom, the obvious model to choose as a basis was the F-4J. At an early stage the decision was taken to switch to Rolls-Royce Spey 202/203 engines, necessitating a redesigned engine bay fed by a new inlet duct about 6in wider, with larger bellmouth nozzles, new inlet and bellmouth control systems, auxiliary rear air doors and re-faired lower rear fuselage. To meet the severe British carrier limitation on length of 54ft the radar was modified so that the complete aerial dish, with the radome, could swing round through 180°. The fire-control was redesignated AWG-11. Internally there were very widespread equipment changes, in autopilot (Elliott), avionics, instruments and systems. To make the F-4K hold altitude after launch from British

Right: On recovery during the same cross-deck operations, another FG.1 neatly takes No 1 wire, the tyres making only the smallest of smoke-puffs./*USN*

Below right: Another arrival aboard big *'Sara'*, this time with the tyres leaving really impressive smoke plumes. By far the most severe stress on the arrester wire comes as the hook hits it, accelerating the heavy wire to something like 170mph in a fraction of a second. /*USN*

Below: No other Phantom version can lift its nose so haughtily as the Phantom FG.1 (F-4K) of the Royal Navy. This is because of its doubly-extensible nose leg, show here to full advantage as an 892 Sqn aircraft is stropped up for cat-launch from USS *Saratoga* during 'cross-deck' operations in October 1969./*USN*

Crowded foredeck of USS *"Independence"*, cluttered with F-4J Phantoms of VF-84 (Jolly Rogers), VF-41 (Ace of Spades), and Bullpup-toting Skyhawks made by the Douglas part of the family./*US Navy Official*

catapults at lower WOD (wind over deck) speeds the
nose leg was made extra-extensible, the extension being doubled from 20in to 40in. Main gears were rated
for 36 000lb landings at 24ft per second sink rate, and
the arrester hook is strengthened. Major airframe portions were made in Britain, including rear fuselage and
tail from BAC and outer wings from Shorts, bringing
total UK content to no less than 40 per cent. First
flight June 1966. Total of 52 delivered 1968-71, of
which 24 went to the Royal Navy and 28 to the RAF.

F-4M Adopted for the RAF in February 1965, upon
cancellation of the P.1154RAF, this version is
designated Phantom FGR.2 in that service and is a
complete multi-role aircraft. Based on the F-4K, it has
no extra-extensible nose leg, catapult provisions or
aileron droops, but introduces anti-skid brakes, HF
and UHF/VHF, strike camera, IFF, and an LCOSS
and completely new Ferranti inertial nav/attack
system. This and other changes gave a total UK content of 45 per cent. The fire-control is the AWG-12,
there are differences in weapon carriage and release, a
fuller complement of electronic-warfare devices, HF
shunt aerial in the fin leading edge, UHF/VHF aerial
in the fin cap, voice recorder, and provision for an
EMI multi-sensor reconnaissance pod or SUU-23 gun
pod on the centreline. First flown in February 1967,
and 118th and last delivered October 1969.

Top left: A dramatic shot of an 892 Sqn aircraft a moment before leaving the deck of HMS *Ark Royal*. Carrying a heavy load of bombs, this FG.1 needs all the help it can get from the increased angle of attack of the fiercely blown wing; the steam catapult has come to the end of its run and the strop has gone slack, but the main oleos are still firmly compressed./*Foss*

Left: Newly arrived from the United States in early 1969, the Phantom FGR.2s of 6 Sqn, RAF ('The Flying Can-openers'), are the scene of round-the-clock activity as air and ground crews at Coningsby get acquainted with the real thing. Behind are Victor tankers of 57 Sqn./*MoD*

Above: A pleasing group of three FGR.2s of 43 Sqn ('The Fighting Cocks') above HMS *Juno*, a *Leander*-class frigate. Fuel plumes are strongly evident./*MoD*

Top left: Ship No 3 of the Thunderbirds, the premier USAF aerobatic team, pictured over the Gateway Center in downtown St Louis, home of the Phantom. Unfortunately the team no longer flies the Phantom, to economise on fuel — but it's a great picture./*MCAIR*

Bottom left: A Phantom F-4C seen in flight with an F-15A Eagle./*MCAIR*

Top: A real combat action shot taken in South East Asia during the US involvement. A battle-worn F-4C pulls g over suspected VC positions in the kind of manoeuvre that led to the slatted wing./*USAF Official*

Above: Pretty as cherry blossom, the first (St Louis-built) F-4EJ poses for the camera. Subsequently Mitsubishi assembled the EJ in Japan./*MCAIR*

Far right: Very matey air-to-air shot of an aircraft of 41 Sqn, Coningsby, taken (not that you can tell) over St Omer in France — site of the biggest maintenance base of the RFC in World War I./*MoD*

Top right: Taking on juice from a Victor of 55 Sqn, based at Marham, is an FGR.2 of 111 Sqn, Strike Command. Nearly 40 years earlier, 'Treble-One' had been the first squadron equipped with the Hurricane./MoD

Centre right: Tidy echelon of 14 Sqn RAF, based at Brüggen, on the German/Dutch frontier. Picture taken in 1973./*MoD*

Below: This FGR.2 belongs to 228 Operational Conversion Unit at RAF Akrotiri, Cyprus, which has had to do a difficult job of peace-keeping as well as instruction. It is wearing real Sparrows and a gun pod./*MoD*

F-4N By the early 1970s scores of the original F-4Bs of the Navy and Marine Corps had far exceeded their design life. It is the most eloquent testimony to their value, even today, that many of these old and rather tired aircraft, from block 12 through block 28, are being rebuilt and also brought up to something approaching F-4J standard, with this designation. (The procedure was first done with successive models of the F-8 Crusader.) The N incorporates several completely new portions of structure and numerous new or updated equipment items such as the helmet-sight Visual Target Acquisition System (VTAS), Sidewinder Expanded Acquisition Mode (SEAM), Auto Altitude Reporting, dogfight computer, air/air IFF, one-way data link and 30 kVA generators. The initial programme, at the Naval Air Rework Facility, NAS North Island (San Diego), involves 178 rebuilds, the first of which flew in February 1973.

F-4S This is the designation of refurbished F-4Js, initially those of the Marine Corps, after passing through a process giving them increased structural strength, longer fatigue life and updated mission equip-

ment. A second recycling through the St Louis works, at a later date, will give all S models the slatted wing — which leads one to conclude that the Navy erred when, after a lot of argument, it decided not to specify the slatted wing for the F-4J at the outset.

This completes the list of Phantom variants for service use as this book goes to press in 1977. There were, of course, numerous proposed versions that never saw the light of day, potentially the most important of which were the swing-wing projects proposed to several customers from 1962 onwards, notably to replace the US Navy F-111B in 1967 and the RAF AFVG in the same year. It is likely that more versions will appear, probably as rebuilds. For example there is as yet no land-based Phantom with pulse-doppler radar, drooped ailerons and slatted tail, and no carrier-based version with an internal gun. Some Phantoms are likely to gain in structural strength, stiffness, or reduced weight, by the incorporation of composite materials (though no Phantom is known ever to have failed catastrophically in flight, despite well over 7 000 000 flight hours pulling up to 12g). Already many Phantoms have flown in regular service with

Top: Tel Aviv must be deafened by this formation of cannon-armed F-4E Phantoms, newly arrived from the United States and already operational with the Heyl Ha'Avir (Israel Defence Force/Air Force)./*Israeli Official*

Above: Against a background of Persian mountains an F-4D of the Imperial Iranian AF (with gun pod) poses for the camera. The IIAF is the biggest user of the Phantom outside the United States.

rudders made of either beryllium or of boron-fibre composites, and even an old F-4 is still sufficiently potent to warrant the most effective refurbishing.

Apart from aircraft in the inventory, more than 150 Phantoms have been used in special research, test and evaluation programmes. The two biggest conversions for such work were the SFCS and CCV. The former was an invaluable tool in finding a Survivable Flight-Control System, and used quad fly-by-wire channels with full authority and no mechanical back-up. First flown on April 29, 1972, this aircraft helped to provide a sufficient bedrock of confidence for General

Dynamics to incorporate such a system into the F-16. The F-4CCV — the same aircraft, but rebuilt — is much more visibly different, for it incorporates Control-Configured Vehicle technology including powered canard foreplanes and direct-lift-control (DLC) outer flap sections. It retains the full-authority fly-by-wire, and has been flying since April 29, 1974. It considerably increases attainable altitude and rates of turn, but has never been envisaged as having immediate relevance to regular F-4 fighters. One is tempted to ask "Why not?", and the answer is that the money is simply not there to do it.

Right: The SFCS (Survivable Flight-Control System) experimental Phantom began life as a USAF RF-4C (71-2200) but was rebuilt with fly-by-wire controls. Later it was rebuilt again as the F-4CCV./*MCAIR*

Below: The most odd-looking Phantom: the CCV (control-configured vehicle) research aircraft, with powered canard foreplanes, direct-lift trailing edge surfaces and full-authority FBW (fly-by-wire). It first flew in this form on April 29, 1974./*MCAIR*

Tactics and Technology

Adoption of the Phantom by the US Air Force was to some degree influenced by the threatening situation in the SEA (south-east Asia) theatre. The notion of 'brushfire wars' had led some experts in the Pentagon to call for a new class of Co-In (counter-insurgent) aircraft, able to lift large loads of ordnance out of short dirt strips, but quite slow and driven by propellers. There was a contrary body of opinion which adhered to the established and capable jet fighter as the best all-round answer to tactical needs; it could be a delivery system against ground targets and also a defender of airspace. Without any dispute, the Phantom was the best multi-role fighter in the world, and it was for this reason that it was produced in much larger numbers, and for much longer, than even Mac expected.

Yet it would be mistaken to regard any hardware as perfect. To some degree the Phantom's outstanding flight performance, radar range and discrimination, ordnance payload, and range and endurance formed such an impressive combination that it seemed churlish to offer criticism. But from the start some Navy and Marine Corps pilots had argued for the inclusion of an internal gun, and when the F-4C joined Tactical Air Command, these murmurings swelled to a noisy hubbub of argument. Though the Air Force had pioneered the concept of the gunless fighter in 1950, with the planning of the F-86D and F-89D, these were pure interceptors which were not intended for dogfighting or ground attack. The interceptor concept was continued with the F-102 and F-106, but all the other Century-series fighters had guns, and used them to the full in both air/air and air/ground operations.

The most experienced fighter pilot in the entire Vietnam war, Col Robin Olds, laid it on the line that 'A fighter without a gun . . . is like an airplane without a wing.' With the chosen policy of accepting the Phantom with minimal modification, all that could be done with the F-4C was hang beneath it one, two or even three external pods carrying the rapid-fire 20mm 'Gatling gun'. Like the gun itself, these pods were

General Electric products; the most common types, the SUU-16A and 23A, weigh about 1 730lb loaded and can fire at up to 6 000rds/min. Even one pod could pour out a withering blast of fire, with high muzzle velocity and great reliability; but, while the gun itself was very accurate, the pylon mounting caused considerable shot-dispersion as a result of airframe and mounting distortion. What pilots wanted was an *internal* gun, on the centreline or close to it. This became urgently needed both for air combat and ground attack.

Such an installation had been studied by McDonnell since the earliest days of the Phantom, and several schemes existed. One had a nose almost identical with that of the RF-4C, with the gun firing out of the front camera port, but the arrangement finally adopted — which was greatly helped by the solid-state APQ-120 radar — retains the original nose and adds the gun in a fairing underneath, inclined slightly downwards and faired at the front by a plastic moulding with a rectangular aperture ahead of the barrel in the '6 o'clock' firing position. This gun was introduced with the F-4E in 1967. It was a godsend to pilots in Vietnam, because not only was it much needed for ground attack but it was also sometimes the *only* way to hit enemy aircraft. The rules of the SE Asia involvement prohibited engagement of any aircraft until it had been 'positively identified visually'. Mere absence of correct IFF reply-codes was not enough. This meant that Phantoms sometimes had to close on the enemy, coming inside Sparrow missile range and then inside Sidewinder range, to make certain of the hostile identity. Without a gun the Phantoms had, in the past, been badly placed; the deficiency cost them all their own advantages and enhanced the enemy's.

There was one other major feature introduced to the Phantom at least partly as a result of experience in air combat in SEA. In its original role as a fleet defence interceptor the Phantom seldom had to perform really hard manoeuvres, and was in any case thought unlikely to enter combat at high gross weights. External tanks would be dropped, and the only load was expected to be Sparrow or Sidewinder missiles. On carrier approach the aircraft would be even lighter, and very far from its stalling angle of attack. For these reasons an unforgiving stalling behaviour was accepted. It was known from the outset that it was un-

Right: The crew of a Phantom FGR.2 of 111 Sqn RAF show off their mount, which wears tanks and Sidewinders. In front are four Sparrows and a 'Gatling pod' (there being no internal gun) with a short length of 20mm belt. The left engine auxiliary door, part-open near the tailplane, is not found on US Phantoms./*UK MoD*

wise to haul back on the stick at low airspeeds, or to attempt violent manoeuvres at high weights, especially below 10 000ft. The result would almost inevitably be a vicious stall and fatal spin right into the ground.

Pilots knew this, and avoided it — but it became harder to avoid. The Air Force missions generally involved flight at higher gross weights and at lower levels, and in the SEA theatre the need to fight MiGs and dodge SAMs soon made the stall-spin characteristic a major problem. Though the Phantom had previously enjoyed one of the lowest — perhaps *the* lowest — accident rates, in relation to flight hours, of any fighter in history, the losses due to stall-spin took a marked turn for the worse. Eventually it surfaced in a Congressional inquiry, which, of course, was in public. Hearings before the House Defense Appropriations Subcommittee in August 1971 elicited the disturbing fact that, at that time, the number of Navy and Marine Corps Phantoms destroyed as a result of what the Department of Defense called this 'bad' characteristic had reached 79, with the loss of 33 crewmen. The Air Force figure (very much higher) was not given. In his evidence, Vice-Admiral Thomas F. Connolly, former Deputy Chief of Naval Operations for Air, said 'We built characteristics into the airplane that make it a better fighter, and we accepted this feature so it won't recover from a fully developed spin very easily ... Quite a few of these stall-spins took place below 10 000 feet by pilots who were either dogfighting clear down to the ground if the fight had started up higher, or were pulling out of an attack. We agree with you that it is something that we have to get better at.'

The senior Air Force witness — General Otto J. Glasser, then Deputy Chief or Staff for R and D — also admitted that the stall-spin problem was 'one of those things that perhaps something ought to be done about'. And, whereas the Navy merely sent out a team of test pilots and educational films to 're-instruct pilots', and judged that it was 'on top of the problem', the Air Force chose to spend $101 million on a modification programme. This involved a redesign of the leading edge, replacing the original blown leading-edge flaps by extremely powerful slats. Called 'manoeuvering slats', these are normally retracted flush against the fixed wing to preserve the original flight performance and specific range. At high angles of attack they automatically extend under hydraulic power, no matter what the indicated airspeed, and thus can be used on the approach, in close air combat or in a transonic weapon delivery. McDonnell Douglas, as the company had become in April 1967, described the slats as providing 'up to 33 per cent more lift', and said they 'put the Phantom well ahead of postulated threats in the important air-to-air combat arena' — which was a rather bold claim.

Above: A specially instrumented F-4B/C (Air Force B) photographed during the first gun-firing trials from Eglin AFB.
The Navy had no requirement to fire guns, so the first trials were run by the Air Force — in this case with two wing pods, spewing cases from the open ejection doors./*USAF*

Left: Primary armament of the F-4B and many later versions comprises four or six Sparrow air to air missiles. This sequence shows how a Sparrow — in this case the left rear — is explosively ejected out of its recess (top). About half a second later its motor ignites (centre), accelerating it away ahead (bottom). In Vietnam the US government imposed rules which made Sparrow seldom usable./*All Rocketdyne*

Centre right. Fitting slats to an existing F-4 is more of a job than might be thought. As this diagram shows, it involves a rebuild of almost the whole primary wing structure.

Bottom right: Given otherwise identical aircraft and pilots, this is how much better a slatted F-4E can turn compared with the hard-winged variety. These are the tightest turns that can be pulled at Mach 0·6 at 10 000ft.

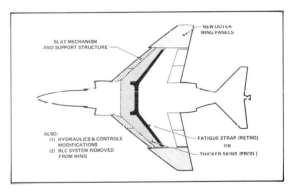

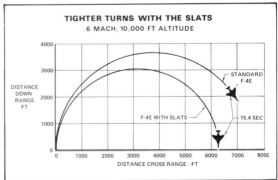

69

Slats were finally introduced to the F-4E line with production block F-4E-48 in June 1972. They have been on every Air Force Phantom since, and on those for some export customers (in fact they were originally developed largely for the F-4F for the Luftwaffe, though this version was delayed until a year after the start of slatted production for the US Air Force). In addition, slats have been retrofitted on nearly every F-4E Phantom in the US Air Force, but not yet to the Navy and Marine Corps Phantoms. There is no doubt they have breathed new life into the capability of what was already a fine aircraft, and helped prolong its production. Incidentally, there is an interesting parallel with the F-86 Sabre, the best fighter of an earlier generation; this entered service with a slatted wing, and later was improved by having the slats removed!

Unfortunately, the slatted Phantom reached the squadrons only towards the end of the American involvement in Vietnam, after it had abundantly proved its worth in exhaustive testing in the United States. But the slat and the internal gun were far from being the only improvements made to the Phantom in the SEA war, because a great deal was done both to equip the aircraft with new devices and to use it in new ways.

The dominant mission of American combat aircraft in that theatre was interdiction, the harassment and destruction of enemy surface forces and supply routes far behind any kind of 'front line'. Sometimes big and scattered targets were subjected to area bombing by B-52 heavy bombers, and both by day and night Forward Air Controllers (FACs) would patrol over designated areas to try to find worthwhile targets or call up airpower to ease pressure on friendly ground forces. There was hardly ever a front line in the accepted sense of the word. Viet Cong guerillas and even the Army of North Vietnam were likely to strike anywhere at any time. Thus airpower had to keep constant watch on the enemy, and the RF-4C with its multi-sensor reconnaissance capability became as important as its ordnance-toting brethren.

This task of finding the enemy was seldom simple. One new tactic resorted to early in the war was aerial defoliation of trees to deny the enemy cover. For years rather unsuitable aircraft were used in difficult and hazardous combat duties, which bore scant resemblance to any mission envisaged when the aircraft was designed. For example, Cessna light planes would carry FACs within rifle-shot distance of the enemy, and big C-130 Hercules transports would orbit for hours at a time directing the air-strike operations of such contrasting aircraft as the B-57, the A-1 Skyraider and the F-4. By 1969 the C-130 was in business on its own account, as the AC-130 gunship, packed with all-weather sensors and guns that poured deadly fire on to ground targets as the gunship orbited round overhead. With similarly equipped versions of the AC-119, these lumbering transports became the No 1 truck-killers in the SEA theatre.

This mention of trucks underlines the vital importance of these vehicles as the equipment item on which the enemy's whole campaign depended. Throughout most of the war the main enemy ports, such as Haiphong, were off-limits to US air power, as were all populated areas such as Hanoi itself. After the bombing raids on North Vietnam were forbidden in 1968 the only way to make a real impression on the enemy was to prevent movement along a fairly short section of the primary supply road, the Ho Chi Minh Trail, in Laos. Here, under a dense leafy canopy, military material poured into South Vietnam. Each truckload could keep action going at a chosen place and time. It became essential to try to halt movement along the road as completely as possible. Only thus could the relentless pressure be taken off the forces of South Vietnam, so that the latter could be strengthened and better trained, in order to take over when the Americans pulled out.

Halting traffic along the Ho Chi Minh Trail became the biggest single task of the airpower in the SEA theatre. Using technology and tactics available in 1965 this objective would have been impossible to attain, but scientists in the Institute for Defense Analyses in Washington had an idea which, after a great deal of development, resulted in completely new technology. It also turned the tables on the aircraft involved, so that Phantoms began to serve as a kind of target marker in order that the big propeller-driven gunships

could rumble in and make the kills! The new system, called Igloo White, was one of several major technical breakthroughs inspired by the challenge of Vietnam.

As the F-4 Phantom was the principal sensor carrier, it is worth explaining how the system worked. The objective was to find troops and trucks coming down the Trail, in all weathers, by day or night. The

Below left: No photograph could better portray the tremendous lifting power of the slatted F-4E wing than this close-up view during an F-4E test from St Louis (airport at right). An Eros pod is clipped on during flight test by McDonnell Douglas as a logical safety measure./*MCAIR*

Below: By 1969 the US involvement in the civil war in Vietnam had led to the expenditure of billions of dollars, many of which were spent on first-class air bases capable of mounting intensive round-the-clock operations. Here is Da Nang AB, S Vietnam (as it then was), with parallel paved 12 000ft runways and extensive modern navaids. The F-4Cs are mainly from the 366th TFW./*USAF*

answer was to 'seed' selected places with sensors, in the same way that an anti-submarine force patterns the sea with sonobuoys. In fact, two of the kinds of sensor, called Acoubuoy and Spikebuoy, were actually derived from sonobuoys but with highly sensitive microphones instead of hydrophones. Each has a camouflaged tube, about 5 inches in diameter and between three and six feet long, carried in multi-round clusters on the F-4 wing pylons. Acoubuoys deployed a parachute to fall gently into jungle foliage, usually thereafter swinging gently from the camouflaged canopy caught in branches. Without radar they were extremely hard to find, and long-life batteries kept each buoy active for days to weeks. In contrast, the free-fall Spikebuoy buried itself in the ground, leaving just its aerial showing. A third sensor, the very widely used Adsid, likewise left only its aerial showing, like a spidery model of a palm tree. This buoy transmitted seismic vibrations caused by trucks and even by people's feet. The fourth buoy, Acousid, could send out both acoustic and seismic information.

All these Igloo White sensors could be controlled by radio signals, with the battery power or the transmitter being switchable on command. When in action, each transmitted any sound or vibration to a relay aircraft. To handle the mass of information, process it in real time so that all the information could be assigned to precise places, and then assess the situation so that aircraft could be assigned to hit the targets, was a huge task calling for many men and computers. It was usually done by a large Infiltration Surveillance Center (ISC), but the larger relay aircraft, such as the

EC-121R Super Constellation, could do this in the air for 12 hours at a time — often in high-threat areas. To try to reduce the cost and effort of maintaining patrols of relay aircraft, small lightplanes were introduced in the Pave Eagle programme. These Beech U-22s could be flown as remotely piloted vehicles (RPVs), but invariably carried a safety pilot.

Right: Though taken as early as 1965 this photograph shows what appears to be already a battered and weary F-4C, leaving its dispersal at Da Nang on a daylight escort mission./*USAF*

Below: Pictures actually over a target are rare. Here is a C-model going flat out directly over a suspected VC position in June 1966. Even in the daytime the problems can be appreciated./*USAF*

Phantoms were the main delivery aircraft of Igloo White sensors. These devices were used by the thousand from December 1967 until the end of the American involvement. The Ho Chi Minh Trail was originally a single road, but by the end of 1970 the logistic routes had become a network covering the whole of eastern Laos. Hundreds of sensors would be operative at any time, and Phantoms would fly in almost every day to seed particular lengths of road — no simple task, because accuracy had to be within the strictly limited range of each sensor, and at low level even a Phantom became very vulnerable. Moreover, it was obviously desirable not to disclose just where the sensors had been placed, so seeding was usually done at night, with the Phantom flying very long distances at tree-top height and releasing the sensors exactly at the positions indicated by its inertial navigator (Navy and Marine Corps Phantoms could not fly such missions, because they lacked an inertial system). Often, extra sensors would be dropped for various reasons. Sensors might indicate passage of a convoy which would then fail to show up on sensors further down the road. The inference was the sudden establishment of a truck park, and extra sensors would be needed to fix its location. As soon as possible the ISC or an EC-121R would mount a strike. The big gunships were laden with radar and IR (infra-red, heat) sensors and could track down their own targets, but the Phantoms had to bomb on inertial positions corresponding to the exact map co-ordinates passed on by the ISC. On receipt of the information, often after take-off, the back-seat man (called the pilot in the Air Force, the front-seater being the aircraft commander) would enter the position in his computer memory. The Phantom would then lay down its ordnance automatically, using wide-area fragmentation bombs or napalm and attacking in a formation spaced so that the ordnance of one aircraft did not damage the next.

Right: One of the many Hobos guided bombs used by the F-4 in SE Asia: a 2 000lb Mk 84 with mid-course DME (distance-measuring equipment) for even better accuracy./*Foss*

Below right: Air-to-air of one of the E models that took part in the October 1973 war, in which 33 Phantoms were lost — almost all of them to Egyptian SAM-6 defence, which caused the Israelis severe problems and forced the West to rethink its ECM capability./*Israeli Official*

Below: A pair of F-4C Phantoms en route to a difficult point target, each carrying tanks and a pair of Mk 84 Hobos bombs./*Foss*

Obviously, such missions called for great crew skill and for fine co-ordination and precision throughout a chain of operators and functioning systems. Yet it achieved effective results, with accuracy at least as good as in visual bombing. On the other hand, Igloo White could be used only against targets that made a noise or vibrated the ground. Many of the Phantom's interdiction objectives were static, and here the problem of finding the target and hitting it was often just as hard. In the earliest Vietnam missions aircraft just bombed visually by day, generally on a map co-ordinate and often with poor results. The introduction of the FAC system greatly improved matters, but the FACs themselves were vulnerable — especially the ones in slow lightplanes — and did not themselves have any sensors. The enemy in the field remained dispersed and highly elusive, while his few predictable major targets became increasingly well defended by intense small-arms fire, guns of up to 85mm calibre, and extremely large numbers of surface/air missiles (SAMs).

Throughout the campaign against South Vietnam the Viet Cong and North Vietnamese army never ceased to build up their anti-aircraft forces, until these were on a scale comparable with those of Nazi Germany. The sheer volume of fire, by both guns and missiles, was often extremely formidable, though it usually lacked quality. In particular, the great numbers

Below: On an air-firing range in southern Germany, a quartet of Luftwaffe F-4Fs let go a shower of napalm tanks./*German Official*

Bottom: Warming up some rather barren, and extremely scorched, earth. Most of the 'napes' have yet to hit./*German Official*

Right: Unlike the Navy, TAC adopted the boom/receptacle method of flight refuelling, to be compatible with SAC's vast fleet of KC-135 tankers. Here three hungry F-4Cs creep up behind the fat tank, whose boomer lies in wait for No 1. In clear air in daylight it is not especially difficult, but . . ./*MCAIR*

of V75SM missile systems (called SA-2 Guideline by the West) did not prove particularly lethal. These are very old weapons, roughly comparable in timing with the obsolete Nike Ajax as far as the specification and design are concerned. They rise from the launcher with relatively slow acceleration, leave a visible rocket trail and have serious deficiencies in structural strength, power of manoeuvre and electronic performance. Skilled F-4 units, working as a team, found it not especially difficult to evade these missiles by a combination of ECM, Wild Weasel activity, anti-radar missiles (Shrike and Standard ARM, homing on the Fan Song radars) and carefully timed violent manoeuvres. The Israeli Heyl Ha'Avir learned the same techniques, though with less electronic help. All this tended to degrade the capability of SAMs as a whole, which was quite unjustified.

Though the old V75SM remained numerically the chief SAM in North Vietnam, with at least 300 mobile and fixed launchers, it was progressively augmented by later and more lethal weapons. Among these were the SA-3 Goa, SA-6 Gainful and close-range Strela (SA-7 Grail), which when properly operated proved to be much more dangerous. Even the old V75SM had indirectly caused the loss of a number of Phantoms through stall-spin accidents resulting from misjudged evasive manoeuvres, and some of the newer missiles

could not be dodged at all — though missile performance did not appear to be precisely repeatable. Both in SE Asia and in the Middle East numerous Phantoms have come up against these later Soviet surface/air missiles, and though details of each encounter are still partly classified it is probably fair to claim that the unassisted aircraft has little chance. Its only hope lies in the liberal use of confusion and deception jamming, decoys and advanced defence-suppression weapons.

In SE Asia the US forces also learned in the hardest possible way (again) that, to hit a difficult point target, free-fall bombs are not enough. Even when released from a platform having the navigation and guidance, sensors, and automatic features of an F-4D, a simple bomb is only too likely to miss by just enough to nullify its effect. From the mid-1960s the US Air Force, and to a lesser degree the Navy and Marine Corps, mounted a tremendous and urgent development programme to equip the F-4 and other tactical aircraft with guided bombs with something akin to pinpoint precision. These are discussed in a later chapter.

All the earliest tactical air/surface missiles were guided by radio command from an operator in the launch aircraft, who had to watch the weapon (which usually carried bright flares) all the way to the target and fly it in the same way one flies an RPV or radio-controlled model aircraft. This was the scheme used in GAM-83 Bullpup, the pioneer US Navy surface-attack missile which was later adopted by the Air Force. Bullpups are still in the active inventory with F-4 squadrons, but most versions are obsolescent. Later the Bulldog, Blue Eye and other developments introduced more automatic forms of guidance, because not even an F-4 wants to hang about close to a heavily defended target while its missile is in flight.

Probably the easiest surface target is a radar, because missiles can be designed to home on the radar's own emissions. In retaliation the radar can be switched off, perhaps as a decoy starts emitting at a safe distance; or, in later sets, they hop from one frequency to another in such a way that no missile can ever lock-on. For non-emitting targets the two guidance methods on which the US forces concentrated their efforts are laser designation and TV guidance. Both are part of the huge field of electro-optics (EO) in which two forms of the same thing, microwaves and visible light, combine to make a missile home on a particular target. In every case the philosophy is 'launch and leave'; once it has released its missile the carrier aircraft can depart from the target area with all speed. Some of the longest-ranged missiles have an autopilot to keep them flying in the general direction of the target. The terminal homing by TV is just like the old radio-command method, except that instead of watching the missile the operator watches a TV screen showing the view from a camera in the nose of the missile. In more advanced EO methods the missile guidance can actually be locked-on to the target, in some cases before launch, so that it can be left to home on the target by itself. With laser guidance a laser in the launch aircraft, in another aircraft, or used by friendly forces on the ground, sends a beam of coherent light to illuminate the target. A laser receiver in the missile senses light diffused away from the target and, by means of a suitable guidance and control system, steers the weapon directly towards the source of the energy.

These very lethal missiles, which were loosely called 'smart bombs', were developed in parallel with much improved methods of navigation. These were too numerous and complex to be described in detail, but were generally intended to update the early (analog) inertial system fitted to the F-4C and F-4D and tie it in with the high local accuracy of the radio navaid Loran. Though archaic in concept, Loran was rapidly extended in US Air Force service in 1965-75, and became of great importance in Vietnam as a primary navaid for manned aircraft and for RPVs. One Loran system was developed explicitly for the F-4D. Called Pave Phantom, it was a navaid for the precision level bombing of unseen targets, a technique which had previously called for Phantoms to formate on an ERB-

Above: At Mildenhall Chief Master Sergeant White does an external check on an F-4D after a 10hr 45min air-refuelled flight from Holloman AFB, New Mexico, 6 880 miles distant./*USAFE*

Right: Almost daily RAF Phantoms have had to scramble to intercept 'Zombies' — long-range Soviet electronics platforms carrying on the ceaseless game of listening and probing. No outfit has had to identify more Soviet machines than 43 Sqn, here formating with a Soviet Navy Tu-95./*MoD*

66 electronic-warfare leadship and drop their bombs on the latter's command. With Pave Phantom the Lear Siegler company linked the inertial system, the Loran receiver and airborne computer to deliver ordnance to either inertial co-ordinates or the Loran time-differences of the target, and to do so even after loss of either the inertial or the Loran input. Of course, the exact position of the target had to be cranked into the system in advance; Pave Phantom could handle up to eight targets in one mission. Another system used on the F-4 was Pave Spectre, in which a pair of AC-130E gunships bristling with avionics guided F-4s to surface targets and, when necessary, illuminated them with laser designators for the Phantom's smart bombs. There were several other 'paveway' systems developed

for the F-4B — Pave Sword, Fire, Spike and Penny and Knife mentioned presently.

To help aircraft penetrate defended airspace it became ever more necessary in the SEA theatre to back up manned attack aircraft not only by their own ECM and penaids (penetration aids) but also by special electronic-warfare aircraft, by jammers and spoofers, by decoys and, ultimately, by RPVs and preprogrammed pilotless decoys either sent ahead of the attacking force or launched by the attackers themselves. Typically, the cost of an attack mission over North Vietnam, and especially in the Hanoi area, was doubled by the need to provide electronic support, the sole exception being in the case of the small Combat Lancer force of F-111A aircraft, deployed to SE Asia in 1968, which carried adequate ECM systems to be self-sufficient. Of course, the Phantom was designed before major tactical ECM systems had matured, and no provision was made for their incorporation. Thus, they were add-on burdens which often had to be carried externally, displacing a tank or ordnance. They are discussed in a later chapter.

This is probably sufficient tactics and technology to drive home the fact that the Vietnam war was far from being one-sided. Without in the least justifying either the original aggression by the Viet Cong or the involvement of the United States, which are quite outside the field of this book, it is a matter of historical fact that missions over North Vietnam and eastern Laos called for the very greatest qualities of courage and professional skill. The next chapter was written by a man who flew Phantoms in that theatre.

Night Mission on the Ho Chi Minh Trail

The author of this chapter is Mark E. Berent, who has now retired from the US Air Force (four days away from becoming a full colonel). He flew two tours in SE Asia and his decorations include the Silver Star, two DFCs, the Bronze Star and numerous Air Medals, as well as the Vietnamese Cross of Gallantry. He commanded the Wolf FAC unit at Ubon RTAFB, but this story is of a typical mission by the 497th TFS, the only all-night-flying unit in the entire theatre, which also operated from Ubon. His mount was an E, with internal gun — and there was a backseater, but when Berent wrote this story for Air Force Magazine *he wanted to put into his own words his own thoughts and feelings.*

It's cool this evening, thank God. The night is beautiful, moody, an easy rain falling. Thunder rumbles comfortably in the distance. Just the right texture to erase the oppressive heat memories of a few hours ago. Strange how the Thai monsoon heat sucks the energy from your mind and body by day, only to restore it by the cool night rain.

I am pleased by the tranquil sights and sounds outside my BOQ room door. Distant ramp lights, glare softened by the rain, glistens the leaves and flowers. The straight-down, light rain splashes gently, nicely on the walkways, on the roads, the roofs. Inside the room I put some slow California swing on the recorder (*You gotta go where you wanta go . . .*) and warm some soup on the hot plate. Warm music, warm smell . . . I am in a different world. (*Do what you wanta, wanta do . . .*) I've left the door open — I like the sound of the rain out there.

Right: Always efficient, the SEA bases had by 1970 acquired a superficial air of permanence as well. Here the F-4Cs of the 37th TFW line up for refuelling from underground hydrants, while the nearest aircraft is checked by its flight crew./*USAF*

A few hours later, slightly after midnight, I am sitting in the cockpit of my airplane. It is a jet fighter, a Phantom, and it's a good airplane. We don't actually get into the thing — we put it on. I am attached to my craft by two hoses, three wires, lap belt, shoulder harness and two calf garters to keep my legs from flailing about in a high-speed bailout. The gear I wear — gun, G-suit, survival vest, parachute harness — is bulky, uncomfortable, and means life or death.

I start the engines, check the myriad of systems — electronic, radar, engine, fire control, navigation — all systems; receive certain information from the control tower, and am ready to taxi. With hand signals we are cleared out of the revetment and down the ramp to the arming area.

I have closed the canopy to keep the rain out, and switch the heavy windscreen blower on and off to hold visibility. I can only keep its hot air on for seconds at a time while on the ground, to prevent cracking the heavy screen. The arming crew, wearing bright colours to indicate their duties, swarm under the plane: electrical continuity — checked; weapons — armed; pins — pulled. Last all-around look-see by the chief — a salute, a thumbs up, we are cleared. God, the rapport between pilot and ground crew — their last sign, thumbs up — they are with me. You see them quivering, straining, bodies poised forwards as they watch *their* airplane take off and leave them.

And we are ready, my craft and I. Throttles forward and outboard, gauges OK, afterburners ignite, nose wheel steering, rudder effective, line speed, rotation speed — we are off, leaving behind only a ripping, tearing, gut noise as we split into the low black overcast, afterburner glow not even visible any more.

Steadily we climb, turning a few degrees, easing stick forward some, trimming, climbing, climbing, then suddenly — on top! On top where the moonlight is so damn marvellously bright and the undercast appears a gently rolling snow-covered field. It's just so clear and good up here, I could fly for ever. This is part of what flying is all about. I surge and strain against my harness, taking a few seconds to stretch and enjoy this privileged sight.

I've already set course to rendezvous with a tanker, to take on more fuel and for my work tonight. We meet after a long cut-off turn, and I nestle under him as he flies his long, delicate boom toward my innards. A slight thump/bump, and I'm receiving. No words — all light signals. Can't even thank the boomer. We cruise silently together for several minutes. Suddenly he snatches it back, a clean break, and I'm cleared, off and away.

Now I turn east and very soon cross the fence far below. Those tanker guys will take you to hell and then come in and pull you right out again with their flying fuel trucks. Hairy work. They're grand guys.

Soon I make radio contact with another craft, a big one, a gunship, painted black and flying very low. Like the proverbial spectre, he wheels and turns just above the guns, the limestone outcropping, called karst, and the mountains — probing, searching with infrared eyes for supply trucks headed south. He has many engines and more guns. His scanner gets something in his scope, and the pilot goes into a steep bank — right over the target. His guns flick and flash, scream and moan, long amber tongues lick the ground, the trail, the trucks. I am there to keep enemy guns off him and to help him kill trucks. Funny — he can see the trucks but not the guns 'til they're on him. I cannot see the trucks but pick the guns up as soon as the first rounds flash out of the muzzles.

Below left: Typical domestic scenery in SEA: officers' quarters at Cam Ranh Bay AB. Accommodation had to deal with extremes of heat, cold and rainfall./*USAF*

Below: Many aircrew lived in comfortable trailers, each with an air-conditioning unit beside the front door. Cam Ranh Bay, June 1967./*USAF*

Inside my cockpit all the lights are off or down to a dim glow, showing just the instruments I need. The headset in my helmet tells me in a crackling, sometimes joking voice the information I must have: how high and how close the nearest karst, target elevation, altimeter setting, safe bailout area, guns, what the other pilot sees on the trails, where he will be when I roll in.

Then, in the blackest of black, he lets out an air-burning flare to float down and illuminate the sharp rising ground. At least then I can mentally photograph the target area. Or he might throw out a big log, a flare marker, that will fall to the ground and give off a steady glow. From that point he will tell me where to strike: fifty metres east, or 100 metres south, or, if there are two logs, hit between the two.

I push the power up now, recheck the weapons settings, gun switches, gunsight setting, airspeed, altitude — roll in! Peering, straining, leaning way forward in harness, trying so hard to pick up the area where I know the target to be — it's so dark down there.

Sometimes when I drop, pass after pass, great fire balls will roll and boil upward and a large, rather rectangular fire will let us know we've hit another supply truck. Then we will probe with firepower all around that truck to find if there are more. Often we will touch off several, their fires outlining the trail or truck park. There are no villages of hooches for miles around; the

locals have been gone for years. They silently stole away the first day those big trucks started plunging down the trails from up north. But there are gun pits down there — pits, holes, reveted sites, guns in caves, guns on the karst, guns on the hills, in the jungles, big ones, little ones.

Many times garden-hose streams of cherry balls will arc and curve up, seeming to float so slowly toward me. Those from the smaller-calibre, rapid-fire quads; and then the big stuff opens up, clip after clip of 37mm and 57mm follow the garden hose, which is trying to pinpoint me like a search-light. Good fire discipline — no one shoots except on command.

But my lights are out, and I'm moving, jinking. The master fire controller down there tries to find me by sound. His rising shells burst harmlessly around me. The heavier stuff in clips of five and seven rounds goes off way behind.

Tonight we are lucky — no 'golden BB'. The golden BB is that one stray shell that gets you. Not always so lucky. One night we had four down in Death Valley — that's just south of Mu Gia Pass. Only got two people out the next day, and that cost a Sandy (A-1) pilot. 'And if the big guns don't get you, the black karst will,' goes the song. It is black, karsty country down there.

Soon I have no more ammunition. We, the gunship and I, gravely thank each other, and I pull up to thirty or so thousand feet, turn my navigation lights back on, and start across the Lao border to my home base. In spite of an air-conditioning system working hard enough to cool a five-room house, I'm sweating. I'm tired. My neck is sore. In fact, I'm sore all over. All those roll-ins and diving pullouts, jinking, craning your head, looking, always looking around, in the cockpit, outside, behind, left, right, up, down. But I am headed home, my aircraft is light and more responsive.

Below: Alert-crews of the 366th TFW ('The Gunfighters') await the call that will send them running from the alert facility to their F-4Ds. From the left, Bob Price, Mike McKinnis and Edgar Jackson. Da Nang, 1969./*USAF*

Below right: Partners of the Phantom in SE Asia were the Fairchild AC-119 and Lockheed AC-130 Hercules Gunships. These little-known battleships of the night sky were filled with sensors and weapons; they did the killing, while the Phantom suppressed the enemy AA fire.

Too quickly I am in the thick, puffy thunder clouds and rain of the southwest monsoon. Wild, the psychedelic green, wiry, and twisty St. Elmo's fire flows liquid and surrealistic on the canopy a few inches away. I am used to it — fascinating. It's comforting, actually, sitting snugged up in the cockpit, harness and lap belt tight, seat lowered, facing a panel of red-glowing instruments, plane buffeting slightly from the storm. Moving without conscious thought, I place the stick and rudder pedals and throttles in this or that position — not so much mechanically moving things, rather just willing the craft to do what I see should be done by what the instruments tell me.

I'm used to flying night missions now. We 'night owls' do feel rather elite, I suppose. We speak of the day pilots in somewhat condescending tones. We have a black pilot who says, 'Well, day pilots are OK, I guess, but I wouldn't want my daughter to *marry* one.' We have all kinds; quiet guys, jokey guys (the Jewish pilot with the fierce black bristly moustache who asks, 'What is a nice Jewish boy like me doing over here, killing Buddhists to make the world safe for Christianity?'), noisy guys, scared guys, whatever. But all of them do their job. I mean night after night they go out and get hammered and hosed, and yet keep right at it. And all that effort, sacrifice, blood going down the tubes. Well, these thoughts aren't going to get me home. This is no time to be thinking about anything but what I'm doing right now.

I call up some people on the ground who are sitting in darkened, blacked-out rooms, staring at phosphorescent screens that are their eyes to the night sky. Radar energy reflecting from me shows them where I am. I flick a switch at their command and trigger an extra burst of energy at them so they have positive identification. By radio they direct me, crisply, clearly, to a point in space and time that another man in another darkened room by a runway watches anxiously. His eyes follow a little electronic bug crawling down a radar screen between two converging lines. His voice tells me how the bug is doing, or how it should be doing. In a flat precise voice the radar controller keeps up a constant patter — "Turn left two degrees . . . approaching glide path . . . prepare to start descent in four miles."

Inside the cockpit I move a few levers and feel the heavy landing gear thud into place and then counteract the nose rise as the flaps grind down. I try to follow his machine-like instructions quite accurately, as I am very near the ground now. More voice, more commands, then a glimmer of approach lights, and suddenly the wet runway is beneath me. I slip over the end, engines whistling a down note as I retard the throttles, and I'm on the ground at last.

If the runway is heavy with rain, I lower a hook to snatch a cable laid across the runway that connects to a friction device on each side. The deceleration throws me violently into my harness as I stop in less than 900 feet from nearly 175 miles per hour. And this is a gut-good feeling.

Then the slow taxi back, the easing of tension, the good feeling. Crew chiefs with lighted wands in their hands direct me where to park; they chock the wheels and signal me with a throat-cutting motion to shut down the engines. Six or seven people gather around the airplane as the engines coast off, and I unstrap and climb down, soaking wet with sweat.

'You OK? How did it go? See anything, get anything?' They want to know these things and they have a right to know. Then they ask, 'How's the airplane?' That concern always last. We confer briefly on this or that device or instrument that needs looking after. And then I tell them what I saw, what I did. They nod, grouped around, swear softly, spit once or twice. They are tough, and it pleases them to hear results.

The crew van arrives, I enter and ride through the rain — smoking a cigarette and becoming thoughtful. It's dark in there, and I need this silent time to myself before going back to the world. We arrive and, with my equipment jangling and thumping about me, I enter the squadron locker room, where there is always easy joking among those who have just come down.

Those that are suiting up are quiet, serious, going

Above: Mission briefings were often small round-table discussions. Participating here are (from left) Lt-Col Gene Levy, Lt Bob Hand, Lt-Col Harry Falls and Capt Fred Deiger. Cam Ranh Bay, December 1968./*USAF*

Above right: Having parked his Cessna O-1E right up close, FAC (Forward Air Controller) Maj Thomas O Manley has a close look at the F-4C of Maj Joseph D Salvucci and Capt Paul H Froeschner at Cam Ranh Bay. Each splinter-proof revetment carried the name of the flight crew and ground crew of its aircraft./*USAF*

over the mission brief in their minds, for once on a night strike they cannot look at maps or notes or weapon settings.

They glance at me and ask how the weather is at The Pass. Did I see any thunderstorms over the Dog's Head? They want to ask about the guns up tonight, but know I'll say how it was without their questioning.

Saw some light ZPU (automatic weapons fire) at The Pass, saw someone getting hosed at Ban Karai, nothing from across the border. Nobody down, quiet night. Now all they have to worry about is thrashing through a couple hundred miles of lousy weather, letting down on instruments and radar into the black karst country and finding their targets. Each pilot has his own thoughts on that.

Me, I'll start warming up once the lethargy of finally being back from a mission drains from me. Funny how the mind/body combination works. You are all hypoed just after you land, then comes a slump, then you're back up again but not as high as you were when you first landed. By now I'm ready for some hot coffee or a drink (sometimes too many), or maybe just letter writing. A lot of what you want to do depends on how the mission went.

I debrief and prepare to leave the squadron. But before I do, I look at the next day's schedule. Is it an escort? Am I leading? Where are we going? What are we carrying? My mind unrolls pictures of mosaics and gun-camera film of the area. Already I'm mechanically preparing for the next mission.

And so it goes — for a year. And I like it. But every so often, especially during your first few months, a little wisp of thought floats up from way deep in your mind when you see the schedule. 'Ah no, not tonight,' you say to yourself. 'Tonight I'm sick — or could be sick. Just really not up to par, you know. Maybe, maybe I shouldn't go.' There's a feeling the premonition that tonight is the night I don't come back. But you go anyhow, and pretty soon you don't think about it much anymore. You just don't give a fat damn. After a while, when you've been there and see what you see, you just want to go fight! To strike back, destroy. And then sometimes you're pensive — every sense savoring each and every sight and sound and smell. Enjoying the camaraderie, the feeling of doing something. Have to watch that camaraderie thing though — don't get too close. You might lose somebody one night and that can mess up your mind. It happens, and when it does, you get all black and karsty inside your head.

I leave the squadron and walk back through the ever-present rain that's running in little rivulets down and off my poncho. The rain glistens off trees and grass and bushes, and a ripping, tearing sound upsets the balance as another black Phantom rises up to pierce the clouds.

Inside a Phantom

Most readers like the outside of a fighter better than the inside; but, without getting too deep in technicalities, we ought to look briefly beneath the skin to see what makes a Phantom tick. And, or course, the source of most of the ticking is the engines.

McDonnell was lucky to have timed the original F4H design just right so that the General Electric J79 could be used from the outset. This was an extremely significant American engine in which new technology resulted in world-beating performance. To improve efficiency a gas turbine needs a high pressure-ratio compressor, but until after 1950 such compressors worked badly. One answer was to split the compressor into front and rear spools, spinning at different speeds. GE adopted another solution: they used a single high-pressure rotor, but made the upstream rows of intermediate stator blades (normally fixed to the casing) adjustable, so that they could be pivoted to exactly the right angular setting for the airflow. Each adjustable row was then linked by an encircling ring of drive-cranks, and finally the rings were connected to a powerful ram moved by the fuel supply. As a result the J79 was slim, light, powerful and efficient. For the Phantom and other supersonic aircraft it was fitted with an afterburner and variable nozzle. Each engine in an early Phantom weighed about 3 600lb, whereas engines of similar power in other American fighters turned the scales at around 5 200lb. This had a bearing on the Phantom's superior performance.

The first Phantoms went into production powered by two J79-2 engines, each rated at a maximum thrust of 16 150lb, considerably greater than the 14 800 or 15 600lb of the previous versions used in the B-58 bomber and F-104 Starfighter. In 1962 the main-production F-4B version received the J79-8, with an improved compressor and other changes, rated at 17 000lb. A year later the Air Force F-4C was powered by the J79-15, similar to the -8 except for having a self-contained cartridge/pneumatic starter, and with the same ratings. In 1966 the F-4J received

the J79-10, most powerful of all J79 versions with 17 900lb thrust gained by further compressor improvements and a turbine with new high-temperature materials. The corresponding Air Force engine is the J79-17, used in the F-4E and all its variants. Phantom production has been mainly responsible for the fact that by 1976 the number of J79 engines delivered had reached approximately 17 000. Many of these have been built by overseas licensees, and MTU in Germany and IHI in Japan are still producing engines for Phantoms. The engine is fed by an automatic variable inlet and the nozzle is centred in a variable bellmouth. A four-man crew can change an engine in two hours.

When Britain threw its own combat aircraft on the scrap-heap in 1964 and 1965 and bought the Phantom, the decision was taken to replace the J79 by the British Rolls-Royce Spey. This was a totally different and much later engine, a two-spool turbofan originally designed for airline transports and later adopted for the Buccaneer low-level attack aircraft. For the Phantom the Spey had to be restressed for supersonic flight, given an afterburner and variable nozzle and changed in other ways. The Phantom also had to be altered, with a wider fuselage and air inlet ducts enlarged to carry up to 204lb/sec airflow instead of 169lb/sec. Rolls tested a fibreglass mock-up of the new inlet system shipped over from St Louis and everything seemed set fair for a Phantom with higher top speed, much greater range, 30 per cent shorter take-off, faster supersonic acceleration, 20 per cent quicker climb to high altitude and faster response to throttle movements. Unfortunately severe trouble was experienced in matching the engine and airframe, with trouble at both the inlet and nozzle; schedules slipped, costs rose, and performance slumped. Today the British Phantoms work well, and with 20 515lb of urge from each engine can hardly fail to be great performers. But if you visit the RAF squadrons they will tell you about 'the biggest, heaviest, most powerful, most costly and slowest Phantoms in the world'.

In terms of dollar value the contribution to the Phantom made by Westinghouse Systems and Technology Divisions is probably as great as that of any other company. From the very start of the project Westinghouse was the prime contractor for the radar

Right: Hawker Siddeley Aviation is the foster-parent responsible for looking after British Phantoms. This photograph was taken at the HSA test base at Holme on Spalding Moor, Yorkshire, on the occasion of the first flight of the EMI reconnaissance pod in 1969./*Hawker Siddeley*

and fire-control system, and the Phantom radar has always been respected as an equipment of exceptional capability. The complete missile control system of early Phantoms is designated Aero 1A. Its main elements are two radars, the APQ-72 and APA-157. The former, derived from the Aero 13 installation of the Skyray interceptor, is a large and powerful X-band set with range and discrimination that were exceptional for the mid-1950s. In its designation, A signifies use in a piloted aircraft, P is the letter meaning a radar and Q denotes that it serves a combination of purposes (of which the main ones are search and track). The APA-157, which uses the same 32 inch dish, is the CW (continuous-wave) illuminating radar for guiding a Sparrow missile. The third element of Aero 1A is the AAA-4 infra-red seeker described later.

As in all Phantom radars, the radome was designed to be swung open and the entire installation pulled forward on telescopic rails for all-round access. After delivering 899 of these radars Westinghouse delivered 1 594 of two considerably refined models, the APQ-100 for the F-4C and APQ-109 for the F-4D. This series culminated in the APQ-120, a completely new all-solid-state radar for the F-4E and its variants. The elimination of vacuum tubes greatly reduced bulk and power consumption, and dramatically improved reliability in the -120, which also had to meet stringent new requirements due to the cannon armament.

By 1956 Westinghouse was working on a new form of radar called a pulse-doppler. One could write a whole library on the PD technique but, briefly, it is the

only way a modern airborne radar can fully meet combat requirements. It is the only way to avoid blind velocities — angular directions where targets cannot be seen — and to reject 'clutter' and either to detect or reject moving targets on the ground. With ground moving targets rejected, it is possible for a high-flying fighter to see a hostile aircraft at tree-top height, and today's missiles can acquire such a target and home on it, giving what is called 'look down, shoot down capability'. Westinghouse's first production PD radar went into a missile, the Bomarc; the second was the APG-59 (G for fire-control), a portion of the AWG-10 missile control system developed for the F-4J. A close relative, with 180° swinging installation on not only the radome but also the aerial, is the AWG-11 in the British Phantom FG.1 (F-4K). The similar AWG-12 equips the Phantom FGR.2 (F-4M). In 1965 McDonnell said these systems would 'significantly increase the British Phantom's air-intercept capability'. The latest of all Phantom radars, described in 1974 as 'the most advanced weapons control system available to the Free World', is the digital AWG-10(A), with greater capability in a close dogfight. It goes into the refitted F-4J (AC) and F-4S.

One of the obvious features of all early Phantoms is the large bullet-like fairing under the nose; this is seen on the F-4B and C (and G conversions). Inside it is the AAA-4 infra-red seeker, a product of ACF Electronics, looking forward through a black hemispherical 'radome' of thermally transparent material. The seeker is incredibly sensitive, and is able

Top left: Nearly all Phantoms are powered by two General Electric J79 afterburning turbojets. On the casing of the compressor, at the left, can be seen the row of bell-cranks that actuate the rows of variable stator vanes that were such a notable feature of this engine. On the right is the variable afterburner nozzle./*GE*

Above left: British Phantoms are powered by the Rolls-Royce Spey 202/203 afterburning turbofan. About seven years later than the J79 in design, the Spey is shorter, slightly heavier and considerably more powerful. In this photograph the inlet is to the right./*R R*

Above: An unusual Phantom payload: the first flight example of the Beech HAST (High Altitude Supersonic Target), with CSD hybrid propulsion system. The F-4 is probably the chief carry-trials aircraft in the Western world./*United Technologies*

Right: Seen from behind, an FG.1 cat-launch still looks dramatic, if only because of the extremely obvious urge of the Spey engines. In this case there is additional interest: snooping up ahead is one of the formidable Soviet gas-turbine warships of the *Kashin* class./*MoD*

to detect a hostile aircraft's infra-red radiation — heat, which moves at the speed of light, both being electromagnetic energy differing only in wavelength — much earlier than the seeker heads of heat-homing close-range air/air missiles such as certain models of Sidewinder and Falcon. In an air/air intercept mode the AAA-4 is used to detect the target, or to acquire the target on command from the radar. It then tells the seeker head of one or more chosen close-combat missiles where to look, slaves them to its own sensitive head, and allows the missile to lock-on and be fired earlier than would otherwise be possible. The seeker does not give range information and is not fitted to later Phantoms with more advanced radar.

Apart from the 500 gallon centreline tanks, the largest store carried by any Phantom is a British product, the EMI reconnaissance pod. Specially developed for the Phantom FGR.2, this contains groups of cameras, the EMI Electronics P331 side-looking radar, and IR with linescan film output. This enables a Phantom to do many of the things performed by the American RF models and still carry a full kit of weapons and nose radar. Another big UK contribution is made by Martin-Baker, whose seats are on every type of Phantom (the current model of seat is the H7). Ferranti, in Scotland, provided the inertial nav/attack system (INS) for British Phantoms, while most other recent versions are fitted with the Litton Industries ASN-63. When Phantoms were staging in large numbers across the Pacific to SE Asia, their INS was proved 'over and over again' (say pilots from Shaw AFB) to be more reliable in course correction than the KC-135 tanker that ostensibly led them

across and solved the navigation problems — though no fighter jock would ever be rude about tankers!

Finally, what about the vital question of armament? From the outset, the main air-to-air armament has always been Sparrow. The basic airframe is made with four deep recesses to carry four of these large missiles semi-flush under the fuselage. A Phantom-size target, if not directly head- or tail-on, can be seen clearly by AWG-10 at a distance of over 40 miles, but though the pilot can plan his interception from this point, he cannot yet launch a missile. As the range closes to less than 15 miles the Sparrow, an AIM-7E2 usually, acquires the target and, at about 12 miles, will be firmly locked-on and can be launched between 12 and eight miles. The US Navy and Air Force has since early 1975 been re-equipping with the AIM-7F, with larger (Hercules solid) rocket motor, bigger continuous-rod warhead (moved forward of the wings) actuated by impact or proximity fuzes, and a new doppler homing radar with smaller seeker head. In Britain HSD has for more than three years been developing an even later Sparrow, XJ521, with a totally solid-state microcircuit homing head by Marconi Space and Defence Systems (a company which also supplied the radar homing and warning for UK Phantoms), and HSD fuze. XJ521, now named Skyflash, has greatly enhanced kill probability at all altitudes and from all directions.

For close dogfighting the standard missile is Sidewinder, made in vast six-figure totals in many versions. In 1976-80 the main production variant will be the completely new AIM-9L version, of which the US Navy expects to buy 3 550 in this period and the

USAF 4 810. One of its obvious differences will be double-delta nose fins (not the same idea as the canards on the French Magic missile, which could also be made compatible with the Phantom), and for the more distant future a completely new follow-on missile

— not the Agile, already flown on an F-4D — will be developed for all the US services. In Britain the advanced SRAAM has been reduced to the level of a technology demonstrator, but firings from air-defence Phantoms are likely and if funding is restored this extremely lethal close-range weapon could later be put to use. In Israel the earlier Shafrir, using Sidewinder technology, is a standard weapon carried by the Phantom.

It is doubtful that any aircraft has carried a greater diversity of air/surface weapons than the Phantom. The original F-4B carried only simple bombs and rockets, but the F-4C added guidance for AGM-12 Bullpup in all its many versions. There followed a later missile by Martin Marietta, AGM-62 Walleye, with pinpoint TV guidance, and triple clusters of the Hughes AGM-65A Maverick with the same guidance. Navy and Marine Corps Phantoms can use the Rockwell AGM-53A Condor, with TV guidance from a range of up to about 60 miles, while missiles homing on to hostile radars include Texas Instruments AGM-45 Shrike, General Dynamics AGM-78 Standard

Left: One has to look twice here to see what is going on. Clipping the stern of *Ark Royal* so close that the two 892 Sqn Phantoms appear to be in some peril, a Soviet missile-armed destroyer — one of the *Kotlin SAM prototype* class — clearly believes in togetherness. Fortunately 'The Ark' was hove-to./*MoD*

Below: A neat instructional display of ordnance carried by the FGR.2 in a 6 Sqn hangar. The aircraft still looks remarkably new after five years./*MoD*

ARM and (not yet in service) Texas Instruments AGM-88A Harm (high-speed anti-radiation missile). These anti-radar missiles form part of the kit of the EF-4C and EF-4E Wild Weasel.

The Phantom has also been the chief carrier of the vast numbers of smart bombs whose principles were outlined earlier. These have been produced by Goodyear Aerospace, Texas Instruments and Rockwell, usually in the form of add-on packages to existing bombs of 500, 750, 2 000 and 3 000lb size. Rockwell's Hobos (HOming BOmb System) comprises an EO or IR seeker package mounted on the nose of the bomb, a set of tail controls, and four long body strakes around the bomb itself joining the guidance to the controls. Some have mid-course DME (photo, page 75). These EO and IR weapons come in two sizes based on the Mk 84 (2 000lb) bomb and M118 (3 000lb). In contrast, Texas Instruments usually add the guidance unit entirely at the front, the two most common Paveway-series smart bombs being KMU-388/B (based on the 500lb Mk 82 GP bomb) and KMU-351/B (Mk 84, 2 000lb). These have been used in extremely large numbers and are still used by TAC F-4 squadrons. The KMU-370B/B (3 000lb M118) is reserved for major targets, and KMU-420 and Pave Storm are smart cluster munitions which strew multiple small bomblets. All these homing bombs are guided by a laser receiver in a characteristic annular-ring nose guidance unit, whose signals are processed and used to drive four canard control fins (tail fins in the case of KMU-342).

To use these weapons with laser homing requires a laser illuminator or designator. Several designators have been used with Phantom ordnance, two being carried by the Phantom itself. The Westinghouse ASQ-153 (Pave Spike) looks like a long white cylinder with a medieval knight's vizor on the front; when the vizor is raised it reveals the optical glass with the laser optics behind it, ready to acquire, lock-on and track targets on the ground even while the Phantom takes evasive action. Philco-Ford's AVQ-10 (Pave Knife) is a bigger pod whose forward section is sharply bent downwards. Inside is a Westinghouse laser designator and also a Dalmo-Victor LLLTV (low-light-level TV) camera, with gyro-stabilisation to keep it on-target no matter which way the aircraft points.

To allow a Phantom to penetrate hostile airspace at all needs such an array of penaids that there is little point in giving their designations (many are listed in the descriptions of Phantom variants). Among penaids carried by Phantoms are noise and deception jammers, dispensed countermeasures (chaff, flares and other packages), RF (radio frequency) warning and homing, missile-launch warners, missile-fuze jammers, real-time warning of hostile RF emitters (both surveillance radar and missile-guidance radar) and some

Top : Possibly the largest item ever routinely carried by a Phantom is the EMI reconnaissance pod that can be slung on the centreline of RAF Phantom FGR.2s. Here is a pod with everything opened up to reveal the cameras, IR linescan and side-looking radar. The two circular ducts carry ram air for cooling./*Hawker Siddeley*

Above : Probably the world's best medium-range air-to-air missile for the 1980s is Skyflash, the American Sparrow airframe containing completely new British guidance, fuzing and other items. Hawker Siddeley Dynamics is now in production, following this successful guided flight on November 25, 1975, at Point Mugu, California. The trials aircraft, a US Navy F-4J, obviously has a well-polished wing./*Hawker Siddeley*

Right: One of the biggest missiles compatible with the Phantom is the Navy AGM-53A Condor, which is nearly 14ft long, weighs 2 130lb and can hit targets 70 miles away. As this trials sequence shows, Condor falls free for two or three seconds before motor ignition./*Foss*

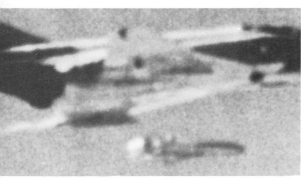

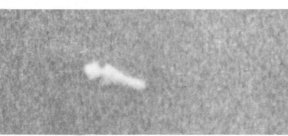

form of control and display system. In several US tactical aircraft such equipment has been packaged internally or in a large bulge or pod carried flush against the fuselage. In almost every case the Phantom has carried penaids in the form of pods on external pylons, the only exception being the purpose-designed EF-4E with its impressive APR-38 installation. Westinghouse, Hughes and Goodyear are among the many big names in ECM and penaids for the Phantom. A quite different passive penaid is the Maxi decoy, carried in boxes of 12 on a wing pylon. Released one by one, the Maxi is a miniature aircraft, made of bronze castings, with flick-open wings spanning 37in. It zooms around in a glide at up to Mach 0·9, with a radar signature like an F-4. Though more effective than mere chaff, Maxis in large numbers pose a dangerous collision hazard!

The only guns used in, or under, Phantoms have been versions of the General Electric Vulcan six-barrel 'Gatling' of 20mm calibre. Prior to the F-4E the gun had to be carried in an external pod. The original pod was the SUU-16A, weighing about 1 720lb with 1 200 rounds. This incorporated an M61A1 gun, driven by a ram-air turbine or, in some installations, by an hydraulic motor. Maximum rate of fire is 6 000 rds/min, but this falls away at low indicated air speed due to reduced turbine power. Most Phantom squadrons have switched to the SUU-23A pod, about 12lb heavier, incorporating the later GAU-4 gun which is self-powered by gas bled from four of the barrels. (An electric inertia starter is used to spin the GAU-4 at the start of each burst.) In the F-4E the GAU-4 is installed with a linkless feed from a drum containing 640 rounds, rather less than in most Vulcan installations. In theory an E could fire its internal gun and three external pods, giving 24 000 shells per minute, without affecting engine operation under any flight condition.

New sensors and new weapons for the Phantom will emerge and reach the squadrons in the near future.

Northrop's **TISEO** (Target Identification System Electro-Optical) is already in use. The main portion is the sensor head, a TV camera with zoom lens packaged in a small pod on the left wing leading edge. It can not only give a clearer visual picture of aerial and ground targets but can also serve an IFF (identification friend of foe) function. In Germany the whopping **MBB Jumbo air-to-surface missile was planned for the F-4, with TV guidance and nuclear or 1 200 lb conventional warhead. In New Mexico flight development is proceeding on the aptly named ERASE (Electromagnetic RAdiation Source Elimination) project,** with a Hughes missile called Brazo by the US Navy and Pave Arm by the Air Force. This missile is intended automatically to home on to the radar of enemy fighters, and the first series of trials from an F-4D against RPV targets scored three out of three. Phantoms will probably one day carry this missile — and learn to use their own radar as little as possible!

Modern defence technology has to move at a cracking pace. Since the above chapter was written, Phantom equipment and external loads have approximately doubled the capabilites of the Elint pods available to Phantom squadrons of the USAF, and the growing list of makers of chaff/jammer/IR dispensed payloads have achieved encouraging advances which unfortunately cannot yet be described. Navigation continues to improve, with Loran ARN-92 already in virtually all F-4Ds and the Lear Siegler ARN-101 digital

Above left: At the NATO Tactical Weapons Meet at Baden Soellingen in June 1974 the RAF Phantom team turned in the highest national score among the seven NATO air forces competing. Here an FGR.2 of 17 Sqn, RAF Brüggen, blasts a ground target with gunfire during the contest./*MoD*

Above right: This FGR.2 of 17 Sqn is seen making the 100th arrested landing at Brüggen. The batsman tells the crew when the wire has slackened and the hook disengaged./*MoD*

Centre left: Another squadron in the RAF Brüggen wing is No 31, one of whose aircraft is pictured going slowly through the decontamination washing plant./*MoD*

Bottom left: Westinghouse has been principal supplier of ECM pods for Phantoms, mounted in a Sparrow recess or hung on a wing pylon. This is a QRC-335A, a forerunner of the mass-produced ALQ-101; about 155 were used by Vietnam F-4 units to provide front and rear radar jamming in E, F and G wavebands./*USAF*

system being retrofitted in the F-4E and RF-4C. It is not yet known whether any Phantoms will be tied into the GPS (Global Positioning System) with worldwide satellite coverage by 1983, which will be used by the F-15 and F-16. Especially big advances have been made in reconnaissance sensors. By the time this book is published the USAF RF-4C force will be equipped with Terec (Tactical Electronic Reconnaissance), using the ALQ-125 system made by Litton Amecom. An advanced Elint, it identifies and locates hostile electronics threats throughout a battle area. A later form, Terec II, will be linked with QSR (Quick Strike Reconnaissance), one of the first multi sensor systems to operate in real time, so that the eventual users of the information get the complete analysis within microseconds of its being detected. The first QSR is being flight-tested in an RF-4C in 1977. This installation has an MTI (moving target indication) radar to cue the FLIR (forward-looking infra-red) Pave Tack pod, from Aeronutronic Ford, which also has a laser designator. Lear Siegler supply a modified ARN-101 Loran C/D with which data are integrated. The next step will be to integrate a new SLAR (side-looking airborne radar) with real-time capability, which at present is known only as UPD-X. Meanwhile Northrop have not rested on their Tiseo laurels (see above) but are adding Latar (Laser Augmented Target Acquisition And Recognition) with narrow-field zoom lens and auto video tracker. What it boils down to is that a Phantom is never the same Phantom two weeks in succession.

Flying the Phantom

The author of this final narrative is another veteran F-4 driver: Henry E. Bielinski. He wrote it as a USAF major for the November 1972 issue of Air Force Magazine, *published by the Air Force Association in Washington DC.*

As we walk up to the Phantom, it seems huge for a fighter. More than sixty feet long and weighing twenty-five tons when configured for a MiG CAP mission, she's not a very pretty sight. Hanging from her belly is a 600-gallon [US gallons] fuel tank, and beneath each wing is a 370-gallon tank. We'll use this fuel on the trip north so that our internal fuel tanks will still be full when it's time to engage MiGs.

Half hidden in the bird's belly are the AIM-7 Sparrow missiles, the basic air-to-air weapons of all models of the F-4. The Sparrow homes on a target painted by the Phantom's radar and gives us the advantage of being able to attack a MiG that is too far away to see.

Under each wing are the infra-red homing missiles used at shorter ranges. The F-4 can carry either the AIM-4 Falcon or the AIM-9 Sidewinder. These give us an intermediate-range capability and can be fired quickly, using only the gun-sight.

Under the nose in a long slender blister is the 20mm cannon, the identifying feature of the E model. It delivers 6,000 rounds a minute, and is deadly in a close-in fight where missiles are useless.

The Phantom's nose is capped by a large radome, housing a radar that is designed to give the F-4 its own GCI capability. The radar will paint targets further out than other Air Force fighters.

Dominating the forward part of the airplane are the

Right: Scramble! Maj Jerome R Barnes beats 1Lt Jack M Brady to their F-4C of the 12th TFW after an alert call. Cam Ranh Bay, 1969. (The name means no disrespect to 'The Thud', the Republic F-105.)/*USAF*

huge airscoops with their hydraulically operated ramps, which limit the airflow at speeds above Mach 1·6, to prevent the engines from choking on supersonic airflow into the turbines.

The wings are semi-delta, with leading and trailing edge flaps. Coupled with these, a boundary layer control system enables the Phantom to operate off relatively short runways. Each wing has a bulge to accommodate the wider wheels required by the Air Force versions of the F-4. The original wheels, designed to operate from steel-decked carriers, were too hard on concrete runways.

The wingtips are bent up to provide more stability at high angles of attack; the horizontal stabiliser is bent to compensate for the bent wing's rolling tendency when the aircraft yaws.

While we are walking around the bird, our Weapon Systems Operator (WSO) is checking out communications gear, inertial navigator, and weapons computers. Using built-in systems, he can check the accuracy of the bombing and missile computers and analyse the functioning of the radar.

The heart of the Phantom's weapons delivery systems is an inertial navigation system (INS). The INS computes air and ground speeds, heading and course, and present location within a completely passive system that cannot be jammed or detected by the enemy.

Using inputs from the INS and the radar, a missile

Above left: Another alert, at Da Nang in December 1971. By this time the greatly improved E was the front-line Phantom. Unafraid of being gobbled up, this pilot was aboard before the photographer could get his name./*USAF*

Above: Front office of an F-4E. Though the APQ-120 display at the top is the same as in the key diagram opposite, this aircraft has a LABS/WPN panel at lower left instead of the missile-status panel, a gun rounds-remaining indicator (bottom, just left of stick), a dual nozzle-position indicator (leaving room for a clock at lower right and a standby attitude director where the clock used to be) and, at upper right, an EROS collision-warning panel./*MCAIR*

Right: Key to the pilot's (front) cockpit of a typical Phantom. Though there were hundreds of detail differences, this drawing would be familiar to any F-4 driver — even to one more used to the British versions. The throttles are on the engine panels 5 and 16, while the stick carries various fire-control and weapon switches./*MCAIR*

PILOT'S COCKPIT
INSTRUMENT ARRANGEMENT

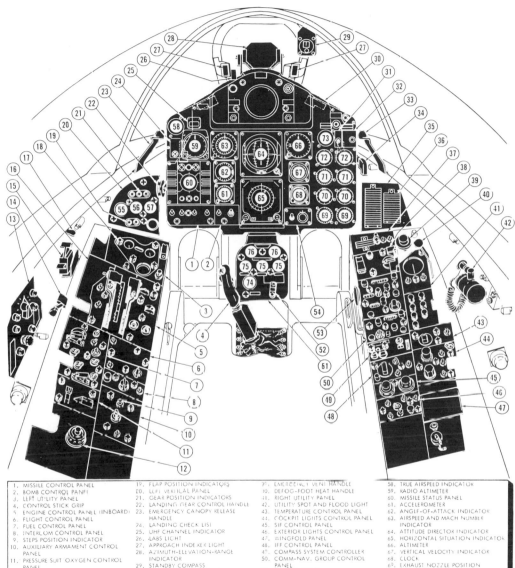

1. MISSILE CONTROL PANEL
2. BOMB CONTROL PANEL
3. LEFT UTILITY PANEL
4. CONTROL STICK GRIP
5. ENGINE CONTROL PANEL (INBOARD)
6. FLIGHT CONTROL PANEL
7. FUEL CONTROL PANEL
8. INTERCOM CONTROL PANEL
9. STEPS POSITION INDICATOR
10. AUXILIARY ARMAMENT CONTROL PANEL
11. PRESSURE SUIT OXYGEN CONTROL PANEL
12. ANTI "G" SUIT CONTROL VALVE
13. RACK CARTRIDGE GROUND TEST PANEL
14. EMERGENCY HYDRAULIC PUMP HANDLE
15. FLAP CONTROLS
16. ENGINE CONTROL PANEL (OUTBOARD)
17. CANOPY CONTROL HANDLE
18. ENGINE CONTROL PANEL (CENTER)

19. FLAP POSITION INDICATORS
20. LEFT VERTICAL PANEL
21. GEAR POSITION INDICATORS
22. LANDING GEAR CONTROL HANDLE
23. EMERGENCY CANOPY RELEASE HANDLE
24. LANDING CHECK LIST
25. UHF CHANNEL INDICATOR
26. LABS LIGHT
27. APPROACH INDEXER LIGHT
28. AZIMUTH-ELEVATION-RANGE INDICATOR
29. STANDBY COMPASS
30. MAIN INSTRUMENT PANEL
31. FEED TANK CHECK LIST
32. TAKE-OFF CHECK LIST
33. MANUAL CANOPY UNLOCK HANDLE
34. ARRESTING GEAR CONTROL HANDLE
35. RIGHT VERTICAL PANEL
36. CAUTION LIGHT PANELS
37. ELECTRICAL CONTROL PANEL
38. T249A BOMB CONTROL MONITOR PANEL

39. EMERGENCY VENT HANDLE
40. DEFOG-FOOT HEAT HANDLE
41. RIGHT UTILITY PANEL
42. UTILITY SPOT AND FLOOD LIGHT
43. TEMPERATURE CONTROL PANEL
44. COCKPIT LIGHTS CONTROL PANEL
45. SIF CONTROL PANEL
46. EXTERIOR LIGHTS CONTROL PANEL
47. WINGFOLD PANEL
48. IFF CONTROL PANEL
49. COMPASS SYSTEM CONTROLLER
50. COMM-NAV. GROUP CONTROL PANEL
51. PEDESTAL PANEL
52. RUDDER PEDAL ADJUSTMENT CRANK
53. EMERGENCY BRAKE HANDLE
54. MODE-BEARING DISTANCE SELECTOR PANEL
55. STABILATOR TRIM POSITION INDICATOR
56. WING TRIM POSITION INDICATOR
57. RUDDER POSITION INDICATOR

58. TRUE AIRSPEED INDICATOR
59. RADIO ALTIMETER
60. MISSILE STATUS PANEL
61. ACCELEROMETER
62. ANGLE-OF-ATTACK INDICATOR
63. AIRSPEED AND MACH NUMBER INDICATOR
64. ATTITUDE DIRECTOR INDICATOR
65. HORIZONTAL SITUATION INDICATOR
66. ALTIMETER
67. VERTICAL VELOCITY INDICATOR
68. CLOCK
69. EXHAUST NOZZLE POSITION INDICATORS
70. EXHAUST GAS TEMPERATURE INDICATORS
71. TACHOMETERS
72. ENGINE FUEL FLOW INDICATORS
73. FUEL QUANTITY INDICATOR
74. PNEUMATIC PRESSURE INDICATORS
75. HYDRAULIC PRESSURE INDICATORS
76. OIL PRESSURE INDICATORS

control computer plots missile maximum and minimum range, lead required, and even points the Sparrow's radar antenna or the IR missile's sensor in the direction of the target.

For air-to-ground munitions, a weapons release computer set (WRCS) will automatically guide the Phantom to a target that can then bombed either blind or visually.

As you strap on the airplane, the first thing you notice are the numerous switches and knobs in the front cockpit, many of which are indistinguishable from each other by touch. To me, the cockpit layout is the biggest limitation of the F-4. When the Air Force decided to buy the Phantom, only absolutely necessary changes from the Navy Fleet Defense Fighter version were allowed. The controls and indicators for the air-to-ground delivery systems were squeezed in wherever there was room.

Starting the Phantom is simple: one switch and one button for each of the J79 engines. On the runway, ready for takeoff, we run up to full military power one at a time because the tires of the F-4 will rotate on the rims if both engines are run above eighty percent power simultaneously. After brake release, we advance power all the way to full afterburner. There is no kick-in-the-pants feeling when the afterburners light on the F-4. It's necessary to check the engine gauges to make sure both burners are actually lit. All you feel is the tremendous acceleration of more than 34 000lb of thrust.

A remarkably short roll — less than 5 500ft with a maximum load — and this giant is in the air. It accelerates so quickly that we must hurry to get gear and flaps up before we reach 250 knots. We're climbing now in military power. There's no fighting for every inch of altitude in this bird. I still get a thrill from watching the earth slide away so quickly.

"We've got a contact thirty degrees right at about eighty miles. Looks level," says the WSO. It must be a tanker or C-130.

Our flight is spread out in loose formation. We check out our infra-red seeking missiles. Got to make sure they're looking in the proper direction.

After checking the missiles, we approach the tanker. Most MiG CAP missions call for refuelling. In the F-4, refuelling is a piece of cake. All you have to do is fly close formation on the tanker while the tanker boom operator jabs a receptacle just behind the WSO's canopy.

With full tanks, we head north. Now, in the relative quiet, we start our switch-setting chores. Switchology is an art all F-4 crews have to learn well if they are to be successful.

And now we're entering MiG country. My eyes stay out of the cockpit, and I only check what's necessary. Fuel is the most important thing.

Enemy radar tracks us every minute, but we must rely mainly on old-fashioned eyeballs. MiG drivers know what will happen to them if they fly where the Phantom's radar can see them, so they will be careful to come from behind.

Our call sign alerts us, and I hear, "... left, at seven-thirty, a little high, two miles, MiG-19 coming this way."

Our whole flight goes into afterburner, jettisons external fuel tanks, and begins a left turn to negate the attack. Since he's been seen this early, the MiG probably won't press in for a missile shot, but our problems aren't over.

MiGs don't fly single ship any more than we do.

Where are his wingmen? Are they in trail a mile and a half behind or coming from the opposite direction, precisely timed by radar so that, no matter which way our flight turns, one of them will be at our six o'clock position? We maintain the turn, looking for the No 2 MiG. There he is, at deep six, a mile and a half. The MiG's controller makes a decision now: which part of our formation to attack? The MiG is positioned best for the other element and goes after it.

To close on the MiG attacking the other element, I push forward on the stick. Now nearly weightless, the F-4 can use all her power to accelerate. I'm consciously feeling for that slight increase in stick pressure which, with my eyes outside the cockpit, is the only indication that we've gone supersonic. The stick actually never moves. The control surfaces are hydraulically operated, and there is no feel in the stick except that which is artificially induced in the control system. However, as the wings go supersonic, the centre of pressure shifts forward ever so slightly, and it takes just a touch of forward stick to make the airplane fly straight ahead.

If you pay very close attention, you can actually feel our F-4 hang up slightly as it goes through the sonic barrier and then accelerate away as we pass through the speed of sound. But in combat this very slight hesitation goes unnoticed. In the back seat, the WSO sees the Machmeter hang slightly and then shoot through Mach 1 as the altimeter winds and then unwinds 2 800 feet—a characteristic of all airplanes going through the Mach. We haven't lost any altitude, but the shock waves on the pitot tube cause changes in the indications.

There are five Gs on our airplane now. I can just feel the onset of buffet as boundary layers of air separate while passing over our wing. This is the point at which the F-4 turns best. If I turn any harder, the drag will become much greater, and, although our nose will swing faster, we'll lose airspeed.

The WSO is trying to get a radar lock-on — we need the radar for range and closure rates. In a turning fight at five Gs, it's very difficult to get that thin pencil beam of our radar dish superimposed on a tiny MiG when the ranges and angles are changing so rapidly. The WSO can't see the MiG at all because it's gone behind the canopy hinge.

I have to be careful because my heavy canopy bows along the sides of the combining glass, and the front of the cockpit could very easily slip into my line of sight and cause me to lose visual contact. Obviously, it's folly for my WSO to keep searching the radarscope; his eyes are needed outside, checking our six o'clock area. We'll have to use the automatic radar acquisition system.

Now my WSO must move two switches and set up up so that our radar will be locked to the sight line. I hit the auto acquisition switch. The radar will now lock-on to the MiG when I put my pipper on it.

We are crossing the circle quickly, and I see that we are already too close for a radar shot. I flip the switch to select my infra-red homing Sidewinders.

Top left: Not a montage but a genuine shot, from the ground, of part of a superb 'Blue Angels' formation. Comment is superfluous./*USN*

Left: Portion of a typical backseater's panel, showing the simple primary instruments mounted above the radar display which is the dominant feature in the back. This panel is in an F-4D; Navy aircraft do not have dual control and have different rear panels./*MCAIR*

Below: Photographer Dennis Robinson, who took this picture of transonic shock vapour at Bentwaters in May 1970, recalls "The FG.1 of 767 Sqn, Yeovilton, put up the best individual aerobatic display I had seen for some time. It terminated with a high-speed horizontal bunt through 360° followed by a roll into a rocketing climb."/*Dennis Robinson*

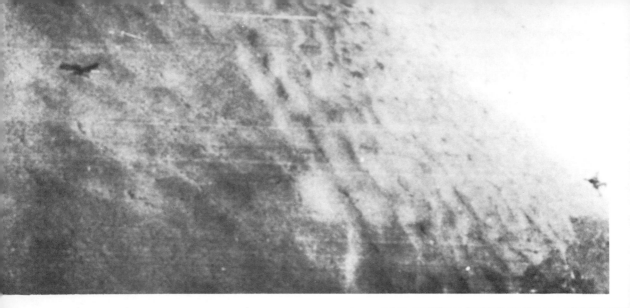

Closing very fast now, I try to manoeuvre into Sidewinder parameters, but I'm facing a dilemma. Without a radar lock-on, my Sidewinders are not looking at the MiG; to put my pipper on him for a radar lock-on, I'll have to slacken my turn and lose the advantage. It's time to forget about missiles and make a cannon attack.

Suddenly I am very sorry I ever hit my auto acquisition switch because every time my radar ranges out, searching for a target somewhere on that radar bore line, my gunsight, computing the 20mm impact point, bounces up and down like it's on a pogo stick. There are two things I can do. I can slide my right hand down the control stick to hit a button that will give me a fixed range input, but with my thumb halfway down the stick grip, it's very difficult to track a small target well and pull the trigger at the same time.

The better solution is to tell my WSO to deactivate the auto acquisition. Still under five Gs, he will have to reach over and move another switch. Now my gunsight is giving me range. I know exactly how big a MiG-19 should look in my gunsight when I squeeze the trigger.

Suddenly, the MiG rolls and begins to dive away, no longer interested in my leader. His radar controller has told him there was somebody moving toward his tail. I begin to go after him. But we've got other problems. Our wingman calls out another MiG.

"Eight o'clock and closing. Break left."

Our problem instantly becomes one of defence.

This time, I pull six and a half Gs. I don't have any qualms about pulling more. I've never heard of the wings coming off an F-4. Three of my buddies have pulled twelve Gs and brought the bird home. If I don't watch my step, we may have a similar story to tell, for we are slowing down.

As we decelerate below Mach 1, still at six and a

half Gs, I feel the tuck — a very slight change in the wing's centre of lift. Now all my senses are alive, waiting for the other tuck — that point where the horizontal stabiliser comes out of the shock wave and regains its effectiveness.

All supersonic fighters have a tucking characteristic, but not necessarily at exactly the same speed or of the same intensity. Suddenly, the stick begins to lighten, and I shove it forward. With no more sensation than a slight bump in an automobile, the tuck is passed. I increase to eight Gs, then finally to eight and a half.

The MiG continues straight ahead. Not having a seventy-five percent chance of a kill, he won't press the attack. He'll be vectored in on some other flight, hoping to catch them unawares.

"Fuel," says the backseater.

We've been manoeuvring in afterburner now for minutes, and although the WSO hasn't got a gauge back there, he knows from experience that we're getting short of fuel. Sure enough it's time to take the formation home.

It may sound as though this incident was a draw, but when you stop to think how many advantages the MiGs had at the beginning — the time, the place, and GCI — the F-4 has done very well indeed. If the MiG and the F-4 were evenly matched airplanes, we could have lost an aircraft today.

Battling other fighters is only part of the F-4 crew's job. The Phantom is also well suited to dealing with the enemy on the ground. The F-4 will carry a heavier ordnance load than most of the strategic bombers of World War II. Shall we take another ride?

Gunship escort is, for me, the most demanding bombing mission flown by the F-4. Flying at night, preferably with no moon, our job is to silence the guns firing at an AC-130 or AC-119 as they fly low and slow, loaded with sophisticated gear to find the enemy along his supply routes.

For the F-4 in the gunship escort mission there are three basic problems: first, keeping the gunship in sight; second, finding a visual reference in a world lit only by starlight; and, finally, flying at maximum endurance—that is, slow, with a heavy load of weapons and fuel.

Keeping the gunship in sight is of primary importance if it is to be protected. And seeing the ground lit only by starlight from the cockpit of an F-4 is no mean task. My lights must be turned down so that they are no brighter than the things we are looking at on the ground.

The WSO's lighting problems are altogether different from mine. He must be able to see the instruments clearly and have enough light to read maps and check lists. His attention is inside the airplane, watching airspeed, altitude, and angle of bank, but he is also concerned with navigation. He must always know our exact location, for in addition to being a talking instrument panel, he is the one who determines target elevation. Fixing our location without being able to see the ground clearly is sporty, to say the least. Dive bombing a gun on a mountaintop, but thinking it's in a valley, could ruin the whole evening!

The gunship is seldom fired upon until it locates a target. Once it finds something, the guns start shooting, and the more vital the target, the more guns to protect it. Now the Phantom pilot's problem becomes one of fixing a gun's position and never moving his eyes from it.

With the target fixed we have to roll in from a slow orbit to a dive bomb pass. Finesse is required during this roll-in. Try to be too quick, and the F-4 goes its own way. I'll lose control only momentarily, but in that moment I'll invariably lose my fix on the enemy gun position.

Assuming all goes well and we're able to roll in, there are still a few details to be considered. Dive bombing usually requires a predetermined angle of dive, a fixed airspeed at release, and a given range to the target. Achieving these at night while trying to roll in from any point on the circle means determining the proper gunsight depression. In the F-4 we have a little piece of magic that makes all these computations for the crew. It's called the dive-toss system, and a well-tuned system will give tremendous accuracy.

My eyes have not moved from the target, and I superimpose the pipper on that spot. Now the WSO must lock the radar to that point on the ground. It's his show until he is locked on and the computer has had time to settle. A good WSO can do it all in two seconds, but when diving into the darkness two seconds is a long, long time.

I usually spend these moments wondering how much distance there is between me and the very hard ground. The WSO and I have been keeping very careful track of our position, and we know what the ground elevation is — if our navigation is correct. We have a radar altimeter, but it only reads up to 5 000 feet. My pressure altimeter is the new and advanced type which requires that I look directly at it to read it. This gauge may be less prone to misinterpretation while flying straight and level in weather, but it is unusable to me on a dive-bomb pass. Right now I'd give three months' pay for the old-fashioned clock-face gauge, with its hands that can be seen in my peripheral vision.

I could use the radar return to judge our altitude, but the radar is turned off in the front seat. Whenever I need the gunsight at night I must not turn on the radar,

because it will ruin my night vision with that eerie glow it casts on the windscreen.

At last my WSO calls, "Clear to pickle," and transfers all his attention to the altimeter. He had

Below: Preparing for the new generation: Westinghouse, builder of the radar in every fighter Phantom, is now using this F-4 to test the advanced multi-mode radar for the General Dynamics F-16./*Westinghouse*

decided how long we'll go before we started this run. Now his only concern is making sure we stick to our plan.

In the front seat, all I have to do is press the bomb button with the pipper exactly on the target. The computer will automatically release our ordnance to hit that point where I put the pipper.

As we recover from the dive, we've got other things to think about. The gunners seldom waste their time trying to hit a fighter in the dark, with one notable exception — at the bottom of a dive-bomb pass. Our only defense is quick turns and high Gs to keep our airplane from flying in a predictable line. The fine art of jinking on instruments is hairy. Now is the time we both hope that the WSO's estimate of the terrain beyond the target is accurate . . .

Back up in orbit, we wait for our next pass. On nights when things are relatively quiet, we may not drop all our bombs before it's time to leave.

One more time on the tanker and then head home. All night landings are on a GCA. It is hard to fly precise instruments in an F-4 with gear and flaps down and bristling with empty bomb racks, but it is easy to stay in the ball park. The bird tends to wallow through the air, and it takes big corrections on the controls to make her change descent or heading, but the power is wonderful. The F-4 is a forgiving airplane for every sin a pilot can commit save one: she will not tolerate much back stick at low airspeed.

The latest Air Force version of the Phantom, the F-4E-48, is a remarkable improvement. Along the leading edge of the F-4E's semi-delta wing is a hydraulically operated slat, providing an increase in turn capability. These new Phantoms are controllable in a full stall, and their low-speed handling characteristics will take much of the thrill out of rolling in on a target at heavy weight and low airspeed.

Equipped with the latest weapons controls located on the instrument panel, and with fewer switches, the pilot spends less time with his eyes in the cockpit. The missile and gun selector switches are located right on the throttles; no more reaching between the knees at five Gs. And there are other minor improvements that, when added to the slats and armament system, make this the best F-4 yet.

The Phantom has proved itself to be a remarkably versatile aircraft. Excelling in the air-superiority role, yet able to deliver ordnance as well as any ground attack plane, it also excels as a high-speed FAC. Never have so many jobs been done so well by a single aircraft at both supersonic and subsonic speeds.

The F-4 will be around for a long time as a mainstay of many air forces around the world. With still further improvements, it will be an even more formidable weapon should the call come for the Phantom to strike again.

F-4E Phantom — Facts and Figures

Designer and Manufacturer	McDonnell Douglas Corp. Basic design done in 1953. First flew on May 27, 1958. F-4E production model, first flew on June 30, 1967
Wingspan	About 38ft 6in
Length	About 63ft
Weight	About 44 000lb, with internal fuel; maximum permissible, near 60 000lb.
Speed	From about 130mph to Mach 2 plus
Service Ceiling	About 60 000ft
Propulsion	Two General Electric J79-GE-17 engines, each with 17 900lb of thrust
Armament	Internal 20mm cannon, 6 000 rounds per minute; radar-guided Sparrow III missiles; infrared, heat-seeking Sidewinder missiles; bombs, rockets
Ferry Range	More than 2 000miles with reserves
Intercept Range	More than 900miles
Air-to-Surface Attack Range	Out more than 100miles in typical high-low mission, depending on bomb loading
Fuel	2 000gallons internal; up to 1 300gallons in three external tanks
Fire Control System	Miniaturised, solid-state AN/APQ-120
STOL Capability	3 000ft or less
World Records	Fifteen, including high- and low-altitude speed; altitude; time-to-climb; transcontinental speed; closed-course speed; and sustained altitude
Sample of Stores Capability	Eighteen 750-lb bombs; fifteen 680-lb mines; eleven 1 000lb bombs; seven smoke bombs; eleven 150gal napalm bombs; four missiles; fifteen air-to-ground rocket packages — in combinations up to eight tons on universal armament racks. Also capable of long-range attack with nuclear weapons and comprehensive penetration aids

107

Phantoms around the World

From its record-breaking youth and arduous battle-proven middle years the Phantom is still only on the threshold of several new careers. Because of its timing the Phantom will have a useful life much longer than that of earlier combat aircraft. It has already been in service as long as the Avro 504, previously holding a place apart when it came to long service use, and will probably go on for as long again. There are several reasons for this. The chief reason is the extremely high cost of modern combat aircraft, far higher even than the rise in price due to inflation, which in combination with generally reduced spending on armaments inescapably means that defence hardware has to have a much longer life than heretofore before it can be replaced. A second factor is that modern combat aircraft are built to last. Their original airframes were designed in the light of new knowledge of fatigue and how it can be avoided, and their engines and systems are also able to go on working for flight-times 50 to 100 times greater than the average flight-times of aircraft in World War 2. A third factor is that the passage of time has not completely outdated the flight performance of the Phantom. It is still an extremely high-performance fighter today, nearly 20 years after it first flew (whereas a Sopwith Camel in 1936 would have found life hard).

Many readers may have wondered if the figures '50 to 100 times greater' were a misprint. They are not. Not only do modern fighters go on flying for much longer lives but they fly far more intensively than their ancestors ever did. This is probably contrary to what might be supposed. It would seem logical for the fighters of, say, World War 2 to have had hectic lives flying combat missions from dawn until dusk, while modern fighters idled their lives away in a financial desert that made such intensive use impossible. Not a bit of it! If we go back just over a decade we find in a McDonnell operational report the news that an F-4C of the USAF 4453rd Combat Crew Training Wing at Davis-Monthan AFB had lately completed 100 flight hours in a single month, in 49 training missions over a period of 28 days. The company was impressed, and added that 100 hours flown by a fighter in one month was 'like a 3:30-minute mile, a round of 55 on the golf course or an 850 three-game series in bowling. It is possible to achieve these goals but not very likely.' Within weeks St Louis was deluged by reports from airfields and carriers around the world showing that hundreds of Phantoms had been regularly exceeding 100 hours a month, logging flight times up to 129 hours.

The contrast between the fighters, and their crews, of today and those of yesteryear are truly dramatic. It is not many years since a fighter pilot with 100 hours on type was a hoary 'old man', a true veteran, to whom the youngsters in the squadron looked up with reverence. Today a Phantom jock may have 100 hours on type before he even gets to a squadron at all, and men with 2,000 hours of Phantom time are just beginning to emerge from the common herd. Time was when a carrier pilot who had made 100 arrested landings in a jet was quite somebody; today 500 arrested landings in a Phantom is peanuts. It has become harder and harder to find yardsticks that are really meaningful or impressive, either in personal careers, in aircraft lives or in unit record-books. Perhaps one thing that will truly impress anyone who was in World War 2 (especially in carrier flying) is to discover the regularity with which Phantom squadrons complete a whole calendar year, racking up 4,000 to 5,000 flight hours in maybe 3,000 missions, without a single aircraft writeoff, and in many cases *without a single aircraft accident of any kind.*

This is eloquent testimony to the robust reliability of the Phantom, the dedication of its servicing crews and the accurate flying of its flight crews. Even on the rare occasions when Phantoms have tragically encountered catastrophic accidents, through no fault of their own, it is remarkable how in many cases the crew have lived to fly again. This is true even of mid-air collisions. During the peak period of the SE Asia involvement there were three collisions between Phantoms and large transport aircraft. On 22 June 1967 a USAF F-4C collided near Saigon with an L-1049H Super Constellation of Airlift flying non-scheduled freight; the Connie crew were killed but both F-4 men punched

Right: This photograph has been cunningly retouched by McDonnell Douglas and may even be a montage; for all that, it gives an exciting impression of a slatted F-4E (equipped as a single-seater for F-4E(F) trials)./*MCAIR*

out safely. On 20 September 1969 another USAF Phantom collided at Da Nang with a DC-4 of Air Vietnam; all five crew and 69 of the 70 passengers aboard the transport were killed, but both men got out of the Phantom. Finally, on 6 June 1971 a Marine Corps F-4B collided over Duarte, California, with a DC-9 of Hughes Air West; the only survivor was one of the Phantom crew. Though one hardly crows with delight over mid-air fatalities, this is the kind of survivability that means much to the man posted to a Phantom squadron.

There is much more one could add about the remarkable toughness of the Phantom, in all its versions. Several have lived to fly again after suffering damage from AA artillery fire and SAMs — often whilst travelling at extremely high indicated airspeed — that would have prevented any other contemporary fighter reaching base. One was repairable after its right wing had been blown off by a 750lb bomb which fell off and detonated at about 100 knots during a heavily laden takeoff. Another returned to base after a cluster of three 500lb bombs had banged into each other and exploded almost immediately after release (these were old bombs designed for release at lower airspeeds, which would have taken longer to unscrew the arming vanes). Of course, any Mach 2 fighter has to be tough, but the Phantom's reputation is legendary.

As I near the end of this book, MAC's team at St Louis are nearing the end of the production line on the Phantom, the longest-lasting fighter production line — in the Western world, at least — since World War 2. McDonnell is today a mature outfit, with an average delivery of 18 jet fighters each month for the past 33 years. These deliveries have wound rather sharply up and down, in the way that bedevils the makers of most kinds of advanced aircraft. At the peak of the SE Asia fighting the St Louis factory was producing 71 Phantoms a month, each of them in terms of man-hours equivalent to about 1½ squadrons of World War 2 fighters. Today the pace has eased, but in July 1976 the plant was still delivering 25 fighters a month — roughly a 50/50 mix of F-4s and the new F-15s. Early in that month the 4,851st Phantom went out of the door, and there are enough on the line to top the magic '5 grand' before the manufacture of new Phantoms comes to an end. Even then St Louis will see Phantoms for many years, because most customers ship them back for modification programmes, structural rework to increase safe flight-time, or for refurbishing for a different customer.

As a result of the Phantom's wide service, McDonnell Douglas and customer air forces have established an extremely large network of supply pipelines, airfields, maintenance facilities, support equipment, and the techniques and experience to use them. The list of Phantom operators has certainly not become final, and several more air forces may be expected to buy new or second-hand Phantoms.

Australia

The RAAF leased 24 F-4E and RF-4E Phantoms from the US Government to help tide it over until delivery of the long-delayed F-111C. The Phantoms equipped Nos 1 and 6 Sqns, and the 23 survivors were ferried back to the United States in 1973-74.

Federal Germany

Of the total of 273, about 260 Phantoms are in front-line service, the remainder being in reserve or written off. The F-4F equips two fighter-interceptor geschwader (wings), JG71 at Wittmundhafen and JG74 at Neuburg. With slightly different avionics and air/ground ordnance the F-4F also equips two fighter-bomber geschwader, JaboG 35 and 36. The complex but unarmed RF-4E equips two reconnaissance wings, AG51 at Bremgarten and AG52 at Leck. Meanwhile, though manufacture of Luftwaffe aircraft was completed early in 1976, German industry continues to build 24 airframe assemblies and several avionic equipments for all remaining new Phantoms, as well as the MTU J79 engine for various customer air forces.

Greece

The Greek government has purchased a substantial number of new Phantoms which form a significant part of the greatly expanded Hellenic Air Force. Within the 28th Tactical Air Command are two Squadrons of F-4Es, one with 18 aircraft and the other with 20, forming 117 Wing at Adravidha. Before the end of 1976 a new reconnaissance squadron was to form, equipped with eight RF-4Es direct from St Louis.

Iran

Ten squadrons of Phantoms, all purchased new, bolster the muscle of the powerful Imperial Iranian Air Force. When this book went to press the IIAF had in service 32 F-4Ds, 141 F-4Es and four RF-4Es, with a further 36 F-4Es and 12 RF-4Es due for delivery by May 1977. These aircraft, with the IIAF F-14 Tomcats, F-16s and F-5E Tiger IIs, are air refuelled by a strategic transport/tanker force of 12 Boeing 707-3J9C and eight ex-TWA 747s, all of which can have Flying Boom and underwing pods for probe/drogue transfers.

Israel

The Heyl Ha'Avir (Israel Defence Force, Air Force) has for several years been a major operator of the Phantom, and has of course used them intensively in actual warfare. The force numbers 204 F-4Es and 12 RF-4Es, with deliveries due to have been completed by January 1977. The F-4E equips six squadrons deployed primarily in the strike role. ECM fit is extensive, and certainly now includes equipment to counter the SA-6 missile with its disconcerting continuous-wave guidance and power of manoeuvre that not even a Phantom can match. It would be logical eventually for Israel to deploy a small force of F-4G electronic-warfare platforms.

Japan

Alone among Phantom operators, the Japan Air Self-Defence Force uses aircraft not assembled at St Louis. The Japanese government signed a complete licence programme including the whole aircraft, engines and selected equipment items. At the time of writing, a total of 128 F-4EJ Phantoms had been budgeted, with about 80 delivered. Three squadrons, Nos 301, 302 and 303, had been fully equipped, No 304 was receiving its aircraft and No 305 was to form in 1977. All five squadrons are part of the 8th Air Wing. A further ten aircraft were budgeted in 1976-77, bringing the total to 138, and a small additional batch is expected to be ordered in the final year, 1977-78.

Singapore

Though no official announcement had been made by late 1976, it is known that the F-4E was the first choice of the Singapore Air Defence Command, and in January 1976 an order for 34 was widely reported unofficially.

South Korea

The Phantom is the most formidable combat aircraft operated by the Republic of Korea Air Force, which might at any moment be plunged once more into furious action by invasion from the north. Two RokAF squadrons each have 18 F-4Es, and two squadrons each have 18 F-4Ds, a total of 72 aircraft all deployed in the attack role. The RokAF reconnaissance type is the small RF-5A.

Spain

Under the terms of a new defence treaty with the United States, 35 ex USAF F-4Cs were supplied to the Ejercito del Aire in 1974, which allotted the EdA designation C-12. Today 34 of these aircraft equip Nos 121 and 122 Sqns at Torrejon, with tanker support from three KC-130H Hercules backed up by ex-USAF KC-97Ls. Before this book is published the C-model Phantoms may have been returned to the United States and replaced by 42 F-4Es. The EDA Phantoms operate in a dual role, tactical attack and air defence, controlled by the Combat Grande air defence system.

Turkey

In 1972 the Turkish government placed an order for 40 new F-4Es, to equip two multi-role squadrons of the Turk Hava Kuvvetleri. About half had been delivered when war broke out with Greece in the summer of 1973, and the US government placed an embargo on arms shipments to Turkey. In late 1975 the ban was lifted, and the full force of 40 is now in service. The US government also offered to supply a further 14 E-models, and as the 1976 budget voted funds for an additional Phantom squadron the offer has doubtless been taken up.

United Kingdom

A total of 170 Spey-powered Phantoms was built for the British government, comprising two prototypes, 48 F-4K (Phantom FG.1) and 120 F-4M (Phantom FGR.2). Except for 28 K-models, for the Royal Navy, all went to the Royal Air Force. About 130 aircraft remain in RAF service, nearly all in Nos 23, 29, 43, 56 and 111 Sqns operating in the air-defence role from Coningsby, Wattisham and Leuchars, plus 228 OCU at Coningsby for crew-conversion. The Royal Navy's sole carrier air group survives aboard *Ark Royal* and includes 892 Sqn equipped with the FG.1. There is no replacement for this carrier when she pays off about 1980, but the air-defence Phantoms of the RAF are to be replaced by the Tornado ADV in the early 1980s.

United States

The Phantom is one of the very few aircraft to have been operated in numbers by the Air Force, Navy and Marine Corps (two others are also McDonnell Douglas products, the A-1 Skyraider and A-4 Skyhawk). By far the biggest operator of the Phantom is USAF Tactical Air Command, with approximately 680 (E, D and a few C-models) equipping 24 squadrons, plus 121 RF-4Cs equipping seven reconnaissance squadrons. Altogether the USAF has about 1,300 F-4D and E Phantoms in the active inventory, equipping 45 squadrons. USAF Europe has seven Tactical Fighter Wings equipped with the Phantom: the 36th TFW at Bitburg, 48 TFW at Lakenheath, 50 TFW at Hahn, 52 TFW at Spangdahlem, 81 TFW at Bentwaters, 86 TFW at Ramstein and 401 TFW at Torrejón. In the Netherlands is a single squadron, the 32 TFS. The RF-4C equips the 10th Tac Recce Wing at Alconbury and the 26th at Zweibrücken. Operating in the air-defence role are the 57th Fighter Interceptor Sqn in Iceland and 154th FI Group in Hawaii. Pacaf (Pacific Air Forces) deploys the 8th TFW in Korea, the 3rd TFW in the Philippines and the 18th TFW at Okinawa, while the 51st Composite Wing in Korea has a mix of F-4s and OV-10 Broncos. Alaskan Air Command includes the 43rd TFS with F-4Es.

The inventory of Phantoms in the US Navy has fallen sharply from the peak in the late 1960s, but still numbers about 220 F-4B, J, N and S deployed in 18 carrier-based squadrons. The Navy does not use reconnaissance Phantoms. About 140 F-4N and S Phantoms, mostly Js, are deployed in 11 squadrons in the three Marine Air Wings, plus 21 RF-4Cs which, with a mix of EA-6A Intruders, equip three electronic and reconnaissance squadrons. There are one squadron of F-4Cs and four squadrons of RF-4Cs in the Air National Guard, and a squadron of F-4Bs in the Marine Air Reserve. Altogether the total US Phantom inventory amounts to about 2,000 aircraft —

easily exceeding any other force of one type of combat aircraft in the West except for the Army's vast inventory of all versions of the 'Huey' helicopter. We shall go on seeing and hearing the tough, jagged, smoky Phantom for a long while yet.

Below: One does not often see a Phantom from quite this angle, and it certainly looks odd. This is a Luftwaffe F-4E, with the tailcone (braking parachute compartment) open.